Lisa,

You were the first to share my story! Thank you for being a great supporter & friend!

Peace, Love &
Many blessings,

# Protected by Purpose

## HOW THE TRANSFORMATION FROM DESPAIR AND HOPELESSNESS CAN LEAD TO AN EXTRAORDINARY LIFE!

**DORINDA WALKER**

# TIMOTHY & TITUS

323 Washington Ave N
Suite 200
Minneapolis, MN 55401

ISBN 978-0-9996450-9-3

**Ordering Information:**
Quantity sales. Special discounts are available on quantity purchases by corporations, associations, and others. For details, please contact Timothy & Titus Special Sales at 612-200-0888.

Manufactured in the United States of America
14 13 12 11 10 9 8 7 6 5 4 3 2 1

Book design by Davida Pitts

This book is dedicated to my children, Janae, Thomas, and Timothy. My proudest joy is being the vessel that God chose to bring you into this world! May your journey into adulthood be filled with love, happiness, peace and many blessings!

Psalm 127:3 - Children are a heritage from the Lord, offspring a reward from him.

# Contents

KEEPING UP WITH THE JONESES  1

HIGH SCHOOL SWEETHEARTS  11

GOD BLESS THE CHILD WHO IS ON HER OWN  19

THE SHATTERING OF A FAMILY  27

HAPPINESS TURNS TO DESPAIR  35

DEVIL IN DISGUISE  45

THE CALM BEFORE THE STORM  57

HEAVEN IS FOR REAL  73

AN UNBEARABLE LIFE  85

FACING MY DEMONS  93

GOD'S ULTIMATUM AND THE BATTLE TO CONTROL  105

GROWN AND FED UP  111

TOUGH LOVE  121

FAITH OVER FEAR  133

THE GIFT OF FORGIVENESS  139

SEVEN LIFE LESSONS  153

# Acknowledgements

First and foremost, I must thank and acknowledge GOD for bestowing so many blessings in my life. I pray that my actions here on this earth demonstrate my appreciation for the love and grace you have provided me.

This book was inspired by my parents who have gone on to shine their bright light in heaven. In spite of the obstacles we endured as a family, my memories of you are filled with the love and joy we shared.

Thomas, my soulmate and life partner, no words can describe how grateful I am for your love and unwavering support. You are the protector of my heart and the fuel that warms my soul.

My extended family, I love and appreciate you! Thank you for trusting me to tell my story and share our family's highs and lows with the world. Our good times certainly outweighed any of the bad. I pray you read this book and find joy in remembering the fond memories shared with our loved ones who have gone on to glory. My intent in writing this book is to help others to heal. I am confident that my parents are proud of this work and what it represents. I hope that you are too!

Dr. Deforest B. Soaries, Jr., there are no words that can accurately express my appreciation for your unwavering belief in me. You challenged me to think bigger, bolder, and to be fearless on this journey. I am so grateful for your mentorship and guidance.

Michele Thornton-Ghee, Deavra Daughtry, Dee Marshall, Sheri Riley, Claudia Chan, Teneshia Jackson-Warner, Cheryl Wood, Cheryl Polote-Williamson, and Felicia Davis thank you for the blueprint. Your work as authors and the empowerment of women has been such an inspiration to me. Your willingness to pour into me, give my voice a platform, and guide me along the way has been invaluable! Much love and continued success to you all!

Latoyia Dennis, when our paths crossed, we had no idea that our corporate connection would turn out to be a purposeful part of God's plan for our lives. We both are required to share our truth to help others. Thank you for the daily calls full of laughter and joy, and for being a constant supporter and spiritual warrior in my life.

Raoul Davis, Leticia Gomez, and Scott Petinga thank you for believing in my story. I am so appreciative of your time and investment in me!

Dr. Holly Carter, Jacque Edmonds Cofer and Salli Richardson Whitfield, thank you for your vision and seeing more than a book. I'm looking forward to our journey in Hollywood. I know it's going to be blessed and brilliant!

We may not talk daily, but I am thankful that our paths crossed on this miraculous journey. My gratitude for what you have deposited into my life is unwavering Sil Lai Abrams, Marshall and Alicia Alston, Jacquelyn Aluotto, Kwaku and Sybil Amuti, Ronald Andrews, Nakia Banister, Tai Bauchamp, Staci Hallmon-Bazzani, Toya Beasley, Vivian Scott Chew, Michael Clark, Cristy Clavijo-Kish, Brandice Daniel, Renau Daniels, Emily Edwards, Dawn Ferguson, Richard Gant, Kenneth Gifford, Nicci Gilbert, Ed Gordon, Yulonda Griffin, Carl Holland, Mark Hug, Monique Jackson, Dawn Kelly, Maurice Kuykendoll, Raymond Lewis, Kristen Maisonable, Yvonne McNair, Pastor Debra Morton, Dele Oladapo, Charlotte Ottley, Dwight Pledger, Monique Porter, Shirley Ann Robertson, Manny Ruiz, Michele Meyer-Shipp, Sidra Smith, Cameka Smith, Phaon Spurlock, Sahieba and Zaida Stevens, Sam Tait, Miguel Thames, Mike Warner, Ronda Williams, Dondre Whitfield, Tirrell D. Whittley and Ernestine Winfrey.

To the many other beautiful and talented tribe of men and women who have supported me in this amazing life, I am so grateful for your friendship, prayers, encouragement and truly humbled by your kindness! ∎

## CHAPTER 1

# Keeping up with the Joneses

THIRTY YEARS AGO, I was a hopeless teenager with no integrity or moral value. I wanted to die and attempted suicide to cope with what I believed to be insurmountable circumstances. As I write this book and reflect on the past two years and the journey that led me to share my story, I must acknowledge the grace and mercy of God. My career affords me the opportunity to travel around the country to support and advocate for the empowerment of underserved communities.

Two years ago, I attended a faith-based conference. The powerful and engaging woman preaching, a prominent bishop, picked me out of the crowd. She advised that she was mesmerized by my presence. She said I had an anointing all over me. I did not know how to respond. I did not consider myself to be religious by any means, although I am a very spiritual being. I most certainly believe there is a higher power that has guided and protected me my entire life. I invited the bishop for tea, and for the first time, I decided to share my story without fear of shame or embarrassment. Her response was, "You should write a book. Your story will help others." I immediately decided to take her advice.

A few months later, I received a call from Dr. DeForest B. Soaries Jr., senior pastor of First Baptist Church of Lincoln Gardens. He asked me to be the keynote speaker at the church's annual Women's Empowerment Luncheon. My initial reaction was fear. I responded, "I'm not a preacher. I won't inspire those women!"

He said, "Dorinda, you are going to bless many by sharing your story. I don't need a preacher. I need you."

I reluctantly agreed. Dr. Soaries has been a mentor and blessing in my life, so I could not say no. In my traditional corporate fashion, I prepared a PowerPoint presentation. I sent it to Dr. Soaries for review. He responded, "Scrap that corporate presentation. Get up there and tell your story." I did, and to my amazement, of the 200 women who attended the luncheon, fifty waited in line for up to an hour to speak with me. I was overwhelmed.

The first woman who approached me said, "No one knows this, but I've been contemplating suicide for the past few weeks; but after hearing your testimony, I know God sent me here. I need help. I know this is not what he wants me to do." I took the time to probe and found out she was contemplating suicide over family drama. I did my best to convince her that she needed to distance herself from her family to find joy. That moment was affirmation. I had to share my story.

A few months later, I was standing on a stage being honored as one of the top twenty-five most influential black women in business. Shortly afterward, I received mention in a Forbes.com article as one of the top black business speakers in the country. Recently, I participated in a photo shoot for *Real Beauty Real Women* to be featured as a top Global Influencer for my advocacy and support of human rights issues and passion for serving and giving back to others. And recently, I received The Honorable

Sheila Jackson Lee Community Service Award and was named one of Houston's top influential business women. Me, a high school dropout, who once had little to no ambition and low self-esteem. As I reflect on the young girl I used to be, I feel nothing but grateful for my journey. A dear colleague once told me, "The will of God will never take you where the grace of God cannot keep you." I never forgot those words of wisdom. It is the only explanation I can fathom. God had a plan and purpose for my life. I believe a part of my purpose is to share my story with you and others. Let me take you through my journey.

I am a descendant of the Jones family, one of the first prominent black families to move to East Orange, New Jersey, in the late 1800s. Our family's legacy of addiction began with my great-grandfather (a black man), who married a woman named Lily D'Elisa (Nana Jones) who emigrated with her family from Castelgrande, Italy, to arrive in Orange, New Jersey, in the early 1900s. Nana Jones was disowned by her family for marrying a black man, which resulted in deep pain and anguish throughout her life. Nana was a pillar of the East Orange community and the glue that held the Jones family together. Even in death, she would become the angel sent to protect me from the darkness.

My great-grandparents had eight children; all but two suffered from addiction including my grandmother Betty, a recovered alcoholic. Although a loving family, the legacy of addiction and dysfunction spread like a plague among the family and ultimately killed my father at the young age of thirty-five.

My memories of Nana Jones are of a kind and loving woman who championed for her family. Nana was stoic, but I could see behind the mask that there was always a deep sadness in her eyes. I believe that sadness stemmed from the heartache of being disowned by her parents for marrying a black man. It also fueled her determination for the Jones family to be a close-knit clan. I know my intolerance of bias and racism stems from her legacy. I can only imagine how different the Jones family legacy could have been if Lily's family had had the compassion and love to embrace her husband and children. Their influence and support may have provided the Jones children more options than a legacy plagued by addiction.

In researching my family history, I discovered that Lily was identified as a white woman until she had children. Upon having biracial children, she was listed as black, although I understand the purpose of the census and why Americans document race. I wish we lived in a world where only one race mattered—the human race. I honor my great-grandmother by advocating for diversity and inclusion and keeping the family-gathering traditions.

When I was young, there was not a week that went by without a family gathering at my aunt Mary's house. Aunt Mary is one of four daughters birthed by Nana Jones. She was married to a handsome, soft-spoken shy man named Chuck. They both had good, honest jobs and worked hard to provide a solid middle-class life for their two sons, David and Trey. My cousin Trey and I were close in age; he is three years my senior. His brother, David, was close in age to my father.

Aunt Mary had all white furniture in her house. She was a neat freak who kept an immaculate but comfortable family home and always wore the signature fragrance of Opium perfume. To this day, whenever I smell that fragrance it reminds me of my beloved Aunt Mary. She was a loud, highly energetic woman, who loved to laugh and have fun, but most of all she loved her family. Although she did not suffer from addiction, she was deeply pained by the addiction that plagued her siblings. She was always the "go-to person" whenever her siblings were arrested or in trouble. My earliest memories of Aunt Mary were her consistent affirmation that I was special. She never spoke negatively about me or my behavior even though there would be plenty of reasons and opportunities to do so in my teenage years. In fact, she was so sure I had a special purpose in life that she would often go toe to toe with other family members who criticized or doubted me. She would scream, "Don't fuck with Dory. She is gonna be somebody. You wait and see!"

My paternal grandparents lived on the second floor of Mary's three-family home. As newlyweds, my cousin David occupied the third floor with his wife. My paternal grandparents, Pop and Betty, also lived a solid middle-class life. My grandfather was a detective for the city of East Orange and my grandmother was a housewife. My grandmother was stunningly beautiful and often compared to Lena Horne. Although she was not as energetic and outspoken as her sister Mary, she was a hell-raiser in her own right. Profanity in the Jones family was the norm. It was almost a term of endearment.

One of my earliest childhood memories of spending time with my grandparents was when my grandfather left his gun on the hamper in the bathroom. I was probably three or four years old, and I walked into the bathroom behind him. I picked up the gun, swinging it as I called out, "Pop, you left your gun, you left your gun." Everybody in the house ducked for cover. My grandfather remained cool and calm, and with his signature grin, he said, "Dory, stop swinging the gun and hand it to me."

I did as he said. He took the gun out of my hand and shook his head. I remember my grandmother's remarks to him as she laughed under her breath, "You dumb motherfucker.

You could have gotten us all killed." My grandfather just put his head down and shook his head. "I know, Betty, I forgot that I left it in the bathroom. It won't happen again."

My cousin Mimi still teases me about that story to this day. Mimi and I grew up like sisters. She is two years older and the only child of my father's oldest sister, Pumpkin. Mimi, Trey, and I were thick as thieves—"The Three Musketeers." We did everything together as youngsters. Every weekend there was a party, we would sneak under the table and watch the grownups party, dance, and drink. My grandmother loved to party. She suffered from alcoholism. Her drink of choice was vodka. I still remember her jumping on top of the table dancing to Al Green's "Let's Stay Together." I remember Aunt Mary being so upset with Pop because every night when he came home from work, he brought a half-gallon of vodka for my grandmother. It wasn't as if he had a choice. If he didn't bring it home, there would be hell to pay.

My grandmother was the oldest of her siblings. She had four brothers, all but one addicted to heroin. She also had two other sisters besides Mary—my aunts Ethel and Essence. Both suffered from addiction. I never met my aunt Essence. Her husband murdered her before I was born. He shot her in front of her sister Ethel and my aunt Courtney, my father's sister, as they were leaving a local tavern. He was enraged because Aunt Essence was in love with another man. He dropped the gun after he shot her and Aunt Ethel picked it up and tried to shoot him, but the gun jammed. Essence left behind two young children. Nana Jones and her daughters stepped in to raise the children along with their paternal grandmother. Essence's husband spent little to no time in jail.

Nana Jones's oldest son, Buck, attempted to retaliate by shooting him. Buck got a call from his dad that Essence's husband was in the local barbershop. Uncle Buck headed to the barbershop with a vengeance and shot right through the window. He failed to kill Essence's husband, but he did move out of the state never to return. He knew that one of the Jones clan would kill him on sight if he were to stay in town. Nothing happened to Uncle Buck. No one in the neighborhood had the nerve to snitch for fear of retaliation by the Jones clan.

Ethel was a true rebel! She dropped out of high school, married a gangster, and had her first child at the age of sixteen. Ethel cussed like a sailor, but she was the most loving and caring woman you could ever meet. Everyone loved her! Mary was overprotective of Ethel and was deeply saddened by her addiction to heroin.

Nana Jones and her three daughters would often get together and cook for the family. We ate delicious Italian and soul food meals. The Jones women were great cooks. In fact, I learned how to cook by watching them in the kitchen. They were also avid soap opera fans who would dress in black whenever a soap character died on the show and cook big meals to commemorate the moment.

The Jones sisters were aunties to many children in the neighborhood, and Nana was the matriarch, a devout Catholic at the helm of the family. Nana's husband was a very dark-skinned man with a prominent mole on his face. He used to sit in the window of their apartment on Park Avenue in East Orange and watch all the happenings on the block. I was told he was abusive to Nana and beat her often in the early years of their marriage. Mary had a love/hate relationship with him. She told me stories about how she would step in the way to take the beatings for her mother. Mary was a fighter through and through.

My uncles told me stories about my great grandfather riding a white horse around town when they were young. There were no sidewalks. He would get high on opium on the weekends and challenge men to fist fights to earn extra money. Apparently, he was a great fighter who rarely lost. Rumor has it that he met Nana while working for her father's bootlegging business. He saw Nana, and they fell madly in love.

Although I've heard really bad stories about his abusive nature, I saw no evidence of it. He would always greet me with a hug, pick me up, and give me Oreo cookies whenever I visited. I remember him being a man of few words. He died when I was five years old. I remember seeing him in the casket and being scared. It was the first time I saw a dead person. My parents forced me to kiss his forehead. The experience traumatized me. Nana Jones saw the look of terror on my face and snatched me out my mother's hands. Nana and I had a connection that I don't completely understand to this day. What I do know is that she was an angel on earth and in heaven. She passed away when I was seven. I remember because we Three Musketeers got in big trouble for playing around at the repast and knocking over the sodas, which resulted in a big mess the Jones sisters had to clean up.

My grandmother Betty has outlived all her siblings, her husband of fifty-three years, and two of her three children. I cannot imagine how she must feel having experienced so much loss in her lifetime. I choose to believe that she has learned to cherish the fond memories to outweigh her grief. ∎

# Dear Reader,

esmond Tutu said it best, "You don't choose your family, they are God's gift to you as you are to them." The Jones women left a great legacy and had a profound impact on my life. They represent strength, courage, and sisterhood, but most of all they represent love. They taught me to accept people for who they are—the good and the bad. To love hard and to cherish the precious time we have here on this earth.

Although I don't have siblings, I choose to honor these women by supporting and uplifting women through the work I do in my career and community. I want a part of my legacy to be an extension of the sisterhood and love I received from these remarkable women. I am sure you stand on the shoulders of someone or many who have had a profound and positive impact on your life. How are you paying it forward? Regardless of your faith and spiritual beliefs, you must understand that universal law dictates that good fortune be bestowed upon people who understand they have an obligation to pay it forward. Are you following universal law or are you stuck on negativity and selfishness? If so, it is not too late. I encourage you to create a list of the people who have had a positive impact on your life and document why. Then assess how you can pay it forward and put in the work to make it happen. Trust me, the reward will be bigger and better than you can ever imagine.

Warm regards,

## CHAPTER 2

# *High School Sweethearts*

THE LOVE STORY OF my parents, Weesee and Bubu, began in high school. Bubu was a light-skinned, tall, and handsome young man, with big, beautiful brown eyes. Although he was popular, he was known as a shy young man of few words and for his love of sports and his distinctive grin. My dad was an all-star athlete. He played football, ran track, and was a great high jumper. His true passion was basketball, and he aspired to make it into the NBA. He is the youngest son of Betty and Pop, loving parents who spoiled him rotten. He was also adored and pampered by his two older sisters, Pumpkin and Courtney. His dad, Pop, was a well-respected narcotics detective and, subsequently, homicide detective for East Orange. He was known for his strong sense of humor, fondness for a cold Budweiser, and love of women, which had a profound impact on the family.

As an adult, I would learn that Pop's infidelity was the fuel that had fired my grandmother's alcoholism. The constant coddling of my father made him ill-prepared to cope with disappointment. In no way do I blame my grandparents for my father's shortcomings. I'm sure they did their best to raise a strong, competent young man. As parents, all we can do is pray that we make the right choices to give our children a solid foundation and the tools and knowledge to achieve success in life.

My mom, Weesee, was a straight-A student with cocoa-brown skin and a huge, curly afro. She was known for her beautiful falsetto voice, small, petite frame, and a smile that would light up any room. She was full of energy, spoke her mind, and was very outgoing. I suspect those qualities were attractive to my dad, given his quiet and shy nature.

My mom is the youngest of six children. Her mother, Molly, was a refined professional woman who worked hard to provide for her children. My mom's dad, Bernard, grew up wealthy but squandered his legacy. Although married to Molly, he was not a model husband. He spent much of his time partying and in the beds of other women. Weesee was extremely close to her siblings but a bit rebellious in following the strict rules of her mother, who worked hard to ensure her kids had every opportunity to receive a college education. My mom was determined to sing and pursue a music career. Although she was a stellar student, she did not yearn to obtain a college degree like her siblings. My mom had an innate gift to absorb and retain information. She was a quick learner and excelled at most anything she chose to do. I'm proud to say I inherited that same gift from my mom, which has propelled me to a lucrative career in corporate America.

My parents met at a party. My mom's best friend was known for giving the best house parties in her parents' basement. Mom would often sneak out of the house to attend, unbeknownst to her parents. Dad was dating my mom's best friend when they met, but as soon as they set eyes on each other, there was an instant love connection. Mom's best friend told me that she could not be mad at the situation. My parents' love for one another was undeniable and unbreakable. My dad's sister Courtney shared an apartment with her husband, and my parents would often visit and use the apartment as their love nest. Mom told me there was an occasion when she got sick and threw up all over Courtney's bed. She said Courtney was livid. Little did she know that my mom was pregnant with me and suffering from morning sickness.

I was born during my mom's senior year of high school. She was seventeen. Mom told me that many people looked down on her due to her teenage pregnancy, but she couldn't have cared less. She was determined to have her child, and she was unapologetic about her love for my dad and the baby that resulted from their bond. Family and friends often reference my strong resemblance to my dad. "Bubu could never doubt you were his child. You are the spitting image of him." I hold this fact as a badge of honor near and dear to my heart.

My dad graduated high school the previous year and joined the Army. He was discovered to be flat-footed in a routine physical and was honorably discharged. Although Pop pushed my father into the armed services in hopes it would steer him away from drug use, both he and Betty were relieved after his discharge because the United States was still in midst of the Vietnam War. The thought of losing their only son in battle was inconceivable.

My parents married in Aunt Mary's backyard upon my dad's discharge from the Army. My father's parents and siblings were not enamored with my mother. They tolerated the relationship because of me and my dad's love for us. The fact of the matter is there would never be any woman good enough for their beloved Bubu. My dad's extended family welcomed and loved my mom with open arms. Their wedding was quite the spectacle on a beautiful summer day. The backyard was filled with family and friends. They exchanged their vows without a hitch and were overjoyed with happiness.

Later in the day, after one too many sips of vodka, Betty began to cuss out Molly. They got into an argument, and Molly and my mom's siblings left abruptly. Aunt Mary was so embarrassed, but she did not dare say anything to Betty. She did scream at Pop for letting Betty get drunk and embarrassing the family. Honestly, it would take way more than that to embarrass the Joneses. The party went on, and my dad made a point to stop by Molly's house to apologize the next day. Molly and my dad were always cordial and pleasant to one another. Both of my grandmothers were strong women. Betty envied Molly for being a strong, independent working woman, and Molly envied Betty for being a well-kept housewife with a husband who doted over her. This is amusing to me, but I do wish they would have taken the time to get to know one another. The two women would have found out they had more in common than they realized. The lesson I learned from experiencing the outcome of their relationship is to never judge a book by its cover. A person may appear to have it all and live a good life, but they most certainly have had, or are experiencing, challenges that those outside of their inner circle will never be privy to. So, I choose not to envy others. Envy is a weight that will only bring the envious down.

My parents were not only beautiful on the outside, they were both caring and loving individuals on the inside. They would both give you the shirt off their backs if anyone asked them to do so. I was told that my father began using drugs because the basketball coach benched him after an altercation the coach had with Pop. This had devastated my dad, and he chose to use heroin to ease the pain and disappointment. It was my dad who introduced my mother to heroin.

Although deeply saddened by this story, I was also disappointed that my dad did not have the courage to pursue his dreams. The one principle my parents instilled in me was to never quit. When I was young, I didn't understand why they were so adamant about this. I now know they didn't want me to follow in their footsteps. I believe if you speak your dreams out into the universe and put in the work, God will put people and opportunities in your life to make those dreams bigger than you could ever imagine. I know this to be true, which is why I never quit or give up on my dreams, and neither should you.

Access to drugs was not difficult to have in the 1970s. In fact, New York City was known as the Heroin Capital of the United States. It was a thirty-minute drive from East Orange. My father's first cousin, Barron, was the high school drug dealer. Barron was one of Ethel and Sean's three sons. He was a handsome, well-dressed, and charismatic young man who was easy on the eyes. He had deep dimples and a striking smile, which made him extremely popular. My generation idolized Barron. He and his dad, Sean, were prominent figures within the Jones clan. Both were known in the streets as flagrant gangsters, but to our family, they were loving and giving individuals who often showered the family with money and lavish gifts. We all knew they acquired money illegally, but no one cared, including Pop. Sean stepped in and served as a father figure to me in my adult years. I remember asking him why he didn't work a regular nine-to-five job. He said, "Baby, I worked at Ford Motor Company for one day. The racist foreman disrespected me, so I hit him over the head with a hammer and ran out of there like a bat out of hell and I never looked back. That's when I knew that working for the man was not for me."

It was not a rare occurrence for a member of the Jones family to get arrested in East Orange. It happened so frequently, Pop would often joke that the Joneses kept him employed. It became a normal occurrence for Pop to step in and assist with the release of a family member. Pop would eventually get me released from jail. You'll read about that later.

My parents were both overjoyed to have a daughter who represented their love for one another, but their love of drugs eventually caused my younger self to succumb to a childhood of sadness, abuse, and low self-esteem. I don't blame or feel shame toward my parents for their addiction. My logical brain understands that addiction is a brain disease. I have read that addiction is comprised of 50 percent genetic predisposition and 50 percent poor coping skills. My heart is broken by the fact that drug addiction cheated my parents from living a joyous life of purpose. They were both beautiful human beings who had much to offer to the world. ■

## Dear Reader,

y father was genetically predisposed to become an addict. His inability to cope with disappointment and the fact that drugs were readily accessible to him facilitated his fate. My mom, on the other hand, would succumb to peer pressure. Her choice and decision to follow my dad in the drug journey turned out to be her biggest regret in life. Unfortunately, this is a story we hear all too often: women blinded by their love of a man, leaving themselves vulnerable to accepting bad behavior and undervaluing their worth. I once read a quote that I often reference when I think about the woman I want to be: "A strong woman is one who feels deeply and loves fiercely. Her tears flow just as abundantly as her laughter . . . A strong woman is both soft and powerful, she is both practical and spiritual . . . A strong woman in her essence is a gift to the world."

Part of my strength comes from learning from the mistakes of my mother, which is why I chose to never use drugs. I knew that if I did, I would become an addict. My childhood was difficult enough. I did not need to add the burden of drug use to my problems. How we as human beings choose to cope with life's disappointments will have not only a profound effect on our own individual lives, but on the lives of those who love and support us. I have no doubt that my dad would have never chosen to use drugs had he known the impact and consequences his addiction would have on his beloved daughter.

Life is guaranteed to provide disappointment and heartbreak. If you choose to react with hopelessness and despair, you are likely to give up and fall victim to the choices and outcomes experienced by my parents. If you respond with courage and a positive attitude to move beyond the grief and disappointment, you most certainly will learn to cope *with difficult situations. The beauty in coping with difficulty is knowing that you will appreciate and be grateful for the good and loving experiences that life is certain to bring your way. The adage "Life is like a roller coaster" is certainly true. How we choose to deal with the ups and downs is up to us. It's in these times, when we have our most defining moments, that our character is shaped.*

*Warm Regards,*

## CHAPTER 3

# God Bless the Child Who Is on Her Own

A S A YOUNGSTER IN the early 1970s, I found joy in being surrounded and euphorically cradled in the arms of those I loved—my parents as well as a multitude of the extended Jones family and friends. One of my first vivid memories of my mom is her singing a song titled "Reasons" by Earth, Wind & Fire, a rhythm and blues ballad released in 1975 on their critically acclaimed album *That's the Way of the World*. My childhood was filled with music. My mother's grandfather owned a music school in Newark, New Jersey, and trained some of the best jazz vocalists in the Tri-State Area. My mom's father, Bernard, instilled a love of music in their household growing up. Her choice of music was eclectic. She loved everything from rock 'n' roll to jazz. My dad loved all the rhythm and blues acts of the 1960s and 1970s, including The Delfonics, The Stylistics, and the Motown Sound. His favorite group was The Whispers. He played and sang every song they ever made on a regular basis during my childhood. At the time, it was a little torturous because he did not have the gift of song—his singing voice was terrible. To this day, if I hear a song from The Whispers on the radio, I can belt out every single lyric.

Aunt Mary's basement was finished with wood panel, plush furniture, a kitchenette, and colorful orange, green, and yellow marble beads that hung in the doorway as you walked in. The décor was hip and stylish for the times. Aunt Mary would cheer and bait my mother on to sing as we gathered in the basement for our typical weekend ritual of family gathering. I remember sitting on my grandmother's lap as the room got quiet while my mom closed her eyes and belted out an amazing rendition of "Reasons." I felt a strong sense of love for my mother at that moment; she was my everything. I was enamored by her beauty and melodic voice. I remember hearing Betty whisper to Ethel, "I don't know where it comes from. She ain't but ninety pounds soaking wet, but that little bitch can sing her ass off." Ethel laughed and said, "You ain't never lied. That's a singing bitch!" and they both chuckled.

One night, the Jones sisters began setting up for the weekly Pokeno game, a game that combines Poker and Keno, very similar to Bingo. The sisters stacked their rolls of nickels in front of them on the card table and picked their game cards before their guests arrived. Pokeno was a serious game for the sisters. They not only placed bets on the first person to get five squares in a row, who was traditionally declared "the winner," they also had mason jars to collect the bets for *Four Corners, Four of a Kind, Center, the letter "X", Round Robin,* and the *House Pot.* A good game would net the host anywhere from fifty to seventy-five dollars, which covered the cost of food and drinks. That was the purpose of the *House Pot.*

Every time a new game started, each player had to put a nickel in every jar. The *House Pot* was given to the host at the close of the game. *Round Robin* was the last game of the night with a cash amount equal to the *House Pot.* The host had the opportunity to determine the requirements to win the pot with the big cash prize. They could state the winner had to get *Center,* or *Four Corners,* or a *Full Board,* etc., to win. The Jones sisters and their friends would rotate host duties so everyone had a chance to earn a few bucks. They would stay up until the crack of dawn playing the game every Friday night.

On the night of this particular game, my parents and a few cousins went outside for about thirty minutes. When they returned, Betty shook her head, rolled her eyes, and sucked her teeth in disgust, sipping on her vodka. My mother had grabbed me out of her lap and began stroking my hair, pressing her cheek to mine, whispering on and off to the lyrics "Tell Me Something Good" by Rufus and Chaka Khan as it played on the record player. Her demeanor and that of those relatives who went outside was very different when they returned to the basement. They couldn't hold their heads up straight. There was a consistent nodding back and forth, and they spoke with a slur. I didn't understand what was wrong, but I knew their behavior was not normal.

Aunt Mary screamed, "Why? Why? Why?" as she pou—nded on the counter.

Ethel replied, "Stop being so damn dramatic, bitch. Chuck, turn up the music. Don't nobody have time for this shit!"

Ethel began straightening up the basement as Mary stormed up the stairs. Chuck and Pop remained quiet. They knew better than to stir the pot with the Jones sisters. They let the tension fade out on its own; albeit, anyone could see the hurt and disappointment in Pop's eyes. He wanted so much more for my dad. Our sober relatives gathered us Three Musketeers up and cheered us on to dance as we held hands in a circle. We were encouraged by the big smiles, love, and laughter in the room. Ethel went upstairs to check on Mary, and they returned with

Nana Jones and food and punch for the kids. They joined in the cheering and laughter as we danced ourselves to sleep. We didn't know it then, but all that dancing was their way of wearing us out so we would not interfere with the Pokeno game.

I loved when my father picked me up and laid my head on his shoulder, trying careful not to wake me. I felt safe, secure, and loved in his arms. I could see and feel his love for me every time our eyes met. I could tell he saw a little of himself in me. He and Pumpkin brought Mimi and me upstairs and put on our pajamas. We crawled into the twin beds in my grandparents' spare room. My dad had a special way of snuggling the covers tight under the mattress to make me feel warm and cozy. I loved when he tucked me in at night.

Aunt Pumpkin was a knockout! She favored her mom, Betty. She had a beautiful smile, hourglass figure, and always dressed like a fashion model. She worked full time and was a cheerleader for the Newark Bears, a semi-pro football team. She also participated in and won a few beauty pageants. She and Mimi's dad parted ways shortly after Mimi was born. His absence was barely recognized because Aunt Pumpkin loved, adored, and spoiled her daughter, and Pop filled in the void of a male role model in both our lives. Aunt Pumpkin never spoke negatively about Mimi's dad. She didn't dwell on his absence. The reality was he gave her the best gift in her life, a beautiful and smart baby girl. I was often mistaken for Pumpkin's daughter by strangers whenever we were out together because we have a lot of the same facial features. I was never bothered by it. She was so beautiful, and I viewed it as a compliment.

Pumpkin used drugs socially in her younger years, though there was never any indication that she had suffered from addiction as a young woman. Unfortunately, she was unable to escape the drug demon as she got older. I noticed the shift right around the age of forty-five. Her long-time boyfriend ended their relationship, and she began using heroin to cope with the devastating breakup. That moment set her on a path that she would never recover from.

The euphoria of those precious family moments was short-lived in my early childhood as my parents' drug use became so overbearing. The safety net I felt in those few loving moments always found a way to collapse. My parents had spurts where they would disappear for days at a time and steal from their parents to feed their addiction. Molly told me that my parents once robbed her house blind, stealing toasters, food, and jewelry. It had gotten so bad that my grandfather Bernard had forbidden them from coming into the house. My mother's brother told me that when I was still in diapers, he got a call from my parents' neighbor, who suspected that I was in the apartment alone.

My uncle stated that when he arrived at our apartment building, he and the neighbor had the superintendent open the door. Sure enough, they found me there alone drinking from the toilet. He scooped me up and brought me to my maternal grandparents' home. At that point, I was shuffled between my grandparents and relatives on a regular basis. Molly worked during the week, so I stayed with Betty, and Pop and Molly would take me on the weekends. My extended family tried their best to fill in the void my parents left in my heart, but no one could ever replace my parents. I would hear the adults say things like, "It's a damn shame how trifling Bubu and Weesee are, running those streets and leaving that baby." I felt rejected.

Did my parents want me? Was I a mistake? I began to feel like I was a burden, so in my young mind, I dared not have a voice or make trouble. If I did, who would take care of me? Who would want me? Although I was never physically abused by my parents, I suffered emotional turmoil because of their addiction. I know it was not their intent, but unfortunately, it is a consequence for children born to drug-addicted parents. There was always a sense of instability and insecurity that resulted in me devaluing my self-worth and developing low self-esteem. You see, my parents thought that leaving me with relatives would ensure that I was safe and taken care of. But they were wrong. The psychological effects of their abandonment are deeply rooted in my psyche. I believe God protected me throughout my life because he knew I felt alone, and I was definitely on my own, even with my extended family around.

Aunt Mary recognized the loneliness in my eyes, which attributed to our connection. She also longed to have a daughter, which never came to be for her. This is why I believe she always doted over me. I represented the daughter she would never have. Mary always affirmed that I was special and destined for greatness. Have you ever been surrounded by family and loved ones and still felt alone? I can completely understand that feeling because I lived it. I watched Aunt Mary spend her life caring for others and neglecting her peace of mind. It literally drove her crazy. ■

# Dear Reader,

n assessing my aunt Mary's life experience, I learned a valuable coping skill. Sometimes you must love people from a distance, a requirement to maintain your own sanity. If you consume your life trying to help people who don't want to help themselves, they will bring you down and stop you from fulfilling your life's purpose. I have committed to never babysit grown folks who know better and yet choose not to do better for themselves. That is not to say that they don't deserve love and support, but there must be boundaries on what you will tolerate. If you are unwavering in upholding standards in your life, people will learn to honor and respect your boundaries.

Here's an example that will help put my advice into perspective: As a kid, did you have a grandmother, aunt, or other relative who you knew not to mess with? You had to be on your best behavior when visiting—you dared not jump on the furniture or misbehave. At the time, you thought they were mean, but looking back on that experience as an adult, you now realize that the relative was not really mean. They had standards and rules for what they would accept when you entered their space. You may not have liked it at the time, but you respected and honored their rules. Peace of mind is something so many of us struggle to attain in life. I encourage you to be unapologetic in doing what you need to do to protect and fill your mind, body, and spirit with positive energy. Sometimes family isn't your friend.

Warm regards,

## CHAPTER 4

# The Shattering of a Family

M Y PARENTS EVENTUALLY LEARNED how to function with their addiction. We lived in a two-bedroom apartment on Munn Avenue in East Orange. My dad worked odd jobs and sold opioid pills to earn income. My mom worked as a legal secretary. I was happy and thriving in kindergarten. My mom made sure that I did my homework every night and practiced my handwriting. She was not a good cook, but she tried her best to make a warm meal each night. I remember telling Nana Jones that my mom cooked spaghetti in a frying pan. She responded, *"Mama mia!"* and threw her hands up in the air, as if it were the end of the world.

My mom could make a mean salad, so she was always assigned salad duty during family gatherings. On occasion, my dad cooked a hearty breakfast of bacon and eggs. He loved to put ketchup on his eggs. I thought it was disgusting. Yuck! Mom ate a loaf of bread each day hoping it would help her gain weight. It never did. She had a naturally high metabolism. Although thin, she was very shapely.

Mom and Dad were friends with a couple who lived around the corner, Bruce and Marie. They would often spend time together in the evenings and on the weekends. I remember one outing, where we all went to the drive-in movie theatre. As we approached the theatre, my dad helped my mom and me into the trunk. They didn't have enough money to pay for the three of us to enter the theatre. My mother held me real tight and told me to be quiet. We both wanted to giggle. I felt like we were on an adventure. Once we were inside, my dad promptly popped the trunk and we jumped in to the backseat of the car. My father purchased popcorn and a soda for us to share.

We always had fun when we were together. There was a lot of laughter and love. Music was always at the forefront in our household. Mom would blast music most of the time. We would dance and sing to songs by popular groups such as the Bee Gees, Wild Cherry, and KC and the Sunshine Band. I let my mom do most of the singing though. I loved to hear her sing. Music was our favorite pastime to occupy ourselves until my dad came home. I could sense how anxious she would be for him to arrive. She watched the clock often. When he opened the door, I would run and scream "Daddy!" as I bearhugged his legs. He'd pick me up into his arms and give me the biggest hug as his face lit up with a huge grin. Both my mom and I were happy to see him come through the door, but for very different reasons.

Dad would come home with my mom's much needed fix. She'd tell me to finish my homework and to read one of my books. "Don't come out until I come get you," she would say sternly. On most nights I would obey. Although my mom was super nice, she was also the disciplinarian of the family. My dad never raised his voice or told me no. The first time my mother spanked me, which was not often, was in my kindergarten year. Aunt Ethel's good friend owned the candy store on the corner by the school. Sometimes

Aunt Ethel picked me up from school and we would stop in the store and she would buy me a snack. One day my mom picked me up from school, and we walked into the store so she could purchase a pack of cigarettes. I walked behind the counter and stuck a few pieces of candy in my pocket without paying, and it went unnoticed.

As we walked down the street, I took the candy out of my pocket and began to unwrap it. I asked my mom if she wanted a piece. She asked me, "Where did you get that candy?"

I replied, "I went behind the counter and took it."

"You did WHAT?!"

She marched me back up the street into the store. She told the owner, "I am so sorry. Dorinda went behind the counter and took some candy without paying. She knows better. Dorinda, give her the candy back and apologize NOW."

I was still trying to figure out why my mother was so mad. In my little five-year-old mind, I had not done anything wrong. I did as my mom said, and I told the owner I was sorry.

The store owner smiled at me and said, "That's okay, baby."

My mom yelled sternly, "Don't you ever take anything from this store without paying, do you hear me? It's stealing, and I will not stand for it." She then proceeded to spank my behind in front of everyone.

I began to cry and scream, "I'm sorry, Mommy. I'm sorry." I was truly more bothered that I had disappointed my mom, than from the spanking. It hurt more mentally than physically. When we got home, I was put on punishment and had to write "I will not steal" 100 times in my notebook and I was not allowed to watch television. My dad never mentioned the incident to me. He entered my room that night, smiled, and shook his head as he tucked me in. The next day, he came home and greeted me with a big hug and a piece of candy.

One night, the melody of my mom's voice humming a familiar tune distracted me, so it was hard for me to obey her orders to stay in my room. I walked into the living room to be closer to her. Unfortunately, the experience I expected was tainted by the vision I saw in front of me. As I walked closer, I saw the back of my dad's head as he sat on the couch, and my mom was facing me. She had a piece of rubber tied tightly around her arm and a bloody hypodermic needle that slipped her grasp and fell from her arm. There was a dirty spoon, a lighter, and white paraphernalia on the table. My mom's head was tilted back and her eyes were closed. She didn't even know I was there. I instinctively knew that my parents did not want me to see this, so I quickly went back into my room and tried to block it all out. Unfortunately, that experience is something that I'll never forget. A few hours later, my dad came to get me, we ate dinner, and my mom ran my bath and put me to bed. My dad came in my room to read to me. He brushed my wild afro into a ponytail and tucked me under my covers nice and snug. This was the typical day in our family life.

One day my mom took me over to Bruce and Marie's apartment. Marie was not home. Bruce and my mom were talking and listening to the radio. My mom rocked me in her arms until I fell asleep. I don't know how long I was asleep, but when I opened my eyes I saw Mr. Bruce and my mother across the room naked. There was drug paraphernalia on the table. I knew my mom being naked with Mr. Bruce was wrong. I quickly closed my eyes and turned over and moaned so they would see that I was waking up. I remember thinking in that moment, *I don't like Mr. Bruce anymore.* Mom gathered her things and shook me gently as I pretended to wake up. When we left the apartment, she was very agitated. She told me not to tell my dad that we had gone to Marie and Bruce's apartment. She started smoking cigarettes one right after the other. I could tell she was upset.

When my dad came into my room to tuck me in that evening, I told him, "Daddy, I saw Mr. Bruce and Mommy naked." He looked stunned. He asked me to explain, so I told him that we went for a visit and what I saw when I woke up. Daddy had tears in his eyes. He asked me if Mr. Bruce put his hands on me.

"No," I said.

He said, "Okay, baby," as he tucked me into bed. He stayed in my room until I fell asleep. I awoke suddenly upon hearing my dad yelling in the next room. My mom was crying and saying that she was sorry. I heard her begging my dad not to leave as they walked toward the front door. I opened my room door and walked toward the hallway. My mom was on her knees holding my dad's legs begging him not to go. He put his bags down and kicked her off his legs. As she got up, he slapped her across the face.

As she fell to the floor, I screamed, "Daddy, please don't go, please!"

He picked up his bags and said, "Sorry, baby, I love you, but I can't stay here with this trifling ho," as he slammed the door behind him. I was devastated. I didn't mean for this to happen. I was too young to really understand the severity of telling my mother's secret. Her infidelity caused my parents to split and left me feeling guilty and abandoned by my father.

My mom never blamed me or spoke of the incident again. She was now alone, battling the demon of addiction with a daughter she had to care for. She could no longer rely on my dad's income, so she did what she had to do to survive. She began stealing meat at the local Kings supermarket to raise money to feed her drug addiction and pay the rent. She sold the meat to those in the neighborhood who paid cash. One day while we were in the supermarket, she told me to make sure no one was looking as she began to stuff her bag with steaks. Suddenly, the manager and two policemen quickly approached us, and we were brought to a room in front of the store. My mom was handcuffed and escorted to the police car. A policeman picked me up and told me I would be okay. He placed me in the backseat of the car with my mother.

She had tears in her eyes and said, "Mommy is so sorry, baby. Don't worry. I called Pop, and he is going to come and get you." When we arrived at the Newark jailhouse, Pop was waiting to take me home. My mother had prior arrests and was sent to the Caldwell Jail Annex to await her day in court. Molly and my mom's siblings were in court awaiting the judge's ruling. No matter how bad things got, my mother knew that Molly and her family would be there by her side. The judge advised my mother that due to her prior arrests and her addiction to drugs, she had two options. She was forced to make a life-changing decision—prison or rehab? She chose rehab. ■

## Dear Reader,

ow ironic that my mom was arrested for doing the same thing she had spanked me for months before, right? She knew stealing was wrong. The same behavior and actions she would not tolerate from me, she could rationalize for herself. Her addiction stripped her of her ability to protect and adhere to her boundaries. She lost her dignity, the love of her life, and now she was in jeopardy of losing her daughter and her freedom. As a woman, I cannot imagine the torment my mom had to endure as she went through this experience. Knowing the spirit who truly lived inside of her, I imagine this caused her a lot of shame and grief.

A lesson that I learned from reflecting on this experience with my mom is that life is guaranteed to put obstacles in your path that will appear to be insurmountable. That drug demon was coming for her hard, but she was not giving up without a fight. She decided to survive the best way she knew how at the time. Unfortunately for her, she made one bad decision after another. Her addiction did not allow her to cope in a rational manner. But most of all, she had no spiritual grounding. The one thing I know for sure is that my parents never spoke to me about God or spirituality when I was young. I believe their lack of faith prevented them from receiving the blessings that could have put them on a different path. When you have faith, a higher power of good will intercede and provide you with the resources to help you overcome.

It took me forty years to really understand the true meaning of faith. It's not about religion. It is your belief that a higher power is in control of your life. It is understanding that you are a servant of that power and your job is to give back and do good upon others. This doesn't mean you must volunteer at the local homeless shelter or donate funds to charitable *organizations. Albeit, these are great ways to give back. It means that your work and actions should provide some type of positive benefit to others.*

*Here's an example: I work in corporate America. I have seen others, and have been guilty of, working hard with the sole goal of being promoted. We tell ourselves, I do a good job, I work hard, I deserve this. Do you see the common theme? It is "I." It's all about the person and not the greater good. Once I began challenging myself by asking, "How is my work? Is it helping others?" I began to make different decisions about how I would navigate my career. I realized that titles and money would not bring me the personal satisfaction I was seeking. When people advised me that they were positively impacted by my work, mentorship, and advice, hearing this brought me joy and personal fulfillment. It is a feeling that money or status cannot buy.*

*When I stopped chasing money and status and began working to truly give back, I was rewarded with promotion, more responsibility, and increased income. You see, I had to prove to that higher power that I was worthy and could be accountable and trusted with these blessings.*

*There's a Bible verse that states: "The one who blesses others is abundantly blessed." Regardless of your religious beliefs, this I know to be true. Drug addicts are misguided by believing they are entitled. It is all about them and their need to get high. The disease of addiction strips them of their ability to cope with reality. It prevents them from approaching life and opportunities from a place of service. They never wake up asking how their actions can help others today. They wake up thinking and planning for how they are going to feed their addiction today.*

*Warm regards,*

# CHAPTER 5

# Happiness Turns to Despair

OLLY TOOK ME TO visit my mom every weekend in rehab. In just a few short weeks, I began to see significant changes in my mother. She was happy, drug free, and full of life. She was cheerleading at the touch football games the men played on the weekends, and she met a new friend named Nicky. They were like the Bobbsey Twins. Nicky and I bonded quickly. We loved each other as if we were family. My mom was content, stress free, and looking forward to leaving rehab to pursue her music career. She had finally found peace. She was also enamored by a very handsome addict named James, whom she had met in the program. He seemed nice, and it was clear that he was infatuated with my mom. James went out of his way to play with me and often told me that he was looking forward to making my mom happy and being part of our family.

During this same time frame, my life began to take a turn for the better. I was reunited with my father, who was now sharing an apartment with his new girlfriend, Mona, and her son, Shane. They welcomed me with open arms. I now had a brother and a real family. Life was good. Shane was younger than me, and I welcomed the opportunity to be a big sister. We enjoyed each other's company. We both wanted siblings, so there were no qualms with us embracing our parents' relationship. I continued to thrive in school, remaining an honor roll and gifted and talented student. Mona adored my dad. She was short and petite like my mom, but more muscular. Although she dabbled with drugs, she didn't let them consume her. She was very responsible, saving money and paying all her bills on time like clockwork. The way she talked about and managed money was intriguing to me, because my parents had really poor spending habits. Neither of them spoke to me about money, savings, or investments. In fact, they both spent money like it grew on trees. Easy come, easy go. I admired the fact that Mona was a strong, hard-working, and self-sufficient woman. Although she loved and adored my dad, she did not depend on him financially.

The happiness we shared was short-lived as life threw my dad a big curveball. His drug use and dealing soon made him the object of a punk beatdown by a "wannabe" gangster named Isaiah. My dad was hustling, chatting it up with some of the guys in the neighborhood. Isaiah was fresh out of jail when he called my dad to his car. Dad was happy to see him. He thought they were friends. When Dad leaned into the car to greet him, Isaiah sucker punched him in the jaw with brass knuckles and broke it. He stated my dad owed him ten dollars. Dad fell to the ground from the impact, and Isaiah raised his fists to hit him again.

Before he could hit my dad a second time, Aunt Ethel appeared out of nowhere screaming, "You punk ass muthafucka! If you hit my nephew again, I will have you and your entire family killed. I promise you that. I dare you to hit him again."

Isaiah knew this was no idle threat given that her sons Barron and Sean Jr. were notorious in the streets for killing anyone who crossed them or their family. In addition, her husband, Sean Sr., was one of the most well-connected drug dealers and numbers runners on the East Coast. Aunt Ethel helped my dad into her car and rushed him to the hospital. As she waited for him to get his jaw wired, she called Aunt Mary to gather the Jones clan at her home.

I remember the night my father and Isaiah had the altercation. Dad came home, and I did not recognize him. He looked like the elephant man. His beautiful face was barely recognizable. Mona, Shane, and I knew that our lives would never be the same. Street code dictates that one of two things would happen: My father had to retaliate to let others know they could not disrespect him, or he could do nothing and establish a reputation as a punk, which would make him fair game for more attacks.

The elder uncles, including Pop, demanded that Isaiah be killed. They had to send a message that the Jones family was off-limits to the streets. My dad was in turmoil for he was no killer. In fact, he never had enemies until that moment. My dad and his cousins arrived at the Palisades lounge, right across from the projects. They walked into the bar.and told Isaiah to step out the back door. Isaiah had no choice. He saw a handful of Joneses spread sporadically throughout the bar with their hands in their pockets, signifying that they were strapped. My dad was in the alleyway planning to shoot Isaiah in the leg in hopes he went down and faked that he was dead.

When Isaiah entered the alley, Barron ordered him to stand on the wall. Barron didn't think my dad would have the heart to pull the trigger, so he was fully prepared to shoot him if need be. My dad could not let the family down. Having never shot a gun before, he aimed for Isaiah's leg.

The pressure from the barrel caused his hand to jump, and he shot Isaiah once in the chest, killing him. Realizing his arrest was eminent, he and his cousins raced to Aunt Mary's house. Mary ordered her husband, Chuck, to get rid of the gun and clothing so the police would have no evidence. Mary told me years later that he threw the evidence into the Hudson River. Mary ensured that I was in the safekeeping of my grandparents. The entire family conspired to get their stories and alibis straight, but my dad was eventually arrested.

Pop couldn't fathom his only son going to prison for an extended period. He called in favors but to no avail. Pop even tried to claim that he committed the murder himself, making headlines in the newspaper. My dad was sentenced to three to five years in prison for aggravated assault.

At this juncture of the story, I'm in second grade. Mary and Betty could no longer coexist under the same roof. I was living with Pop and Betty in their new apartment in Irvington, New Jersey, along with Pumpkin and Mimi. The Jones family was in mourning due to the passing of their beloved matriarch, Nana Jones. Pumpkin was working hard and showering Mimi with designer clothes and the best that money could buy. I was wearing Betty's polyester pants and the hand-me-downs that were provided for me. I felt resentful and angry inside. When I spoke up, Betty told me I was lucky to have clothes on my back and to be appreciative. "Tell your junkie ass mother to buy you some clothes." I felt like a second-class citizen. I began to secretly envy Mimi and the bond she had with her mother. This was the beginning of me believing that I had to please everyone to be liked and loved.

I was a good student, always being the first to raise my hand. I enjoyed learning new things. Although I was shy, I was a very competitive student in class. I kept my head down in school and tried my best to impress the teacher by being smart and well-behaved. I was befriended by a curly, red-headed Jewish boy named Adam. He and I were thick as thieves and played together during recess every day at school. The children who attended the school were predominantly white. It did not phase me at all, because I did not understand that I was viewed differently because of my race. Adam and I did not see ourselves as dissimilar, but we were in for a rude awakening.

One day on the playground, a posse of girls surrounded us. They began pushing Adam and calling him a "nigger lover." He did not fight back. I didn't know what the word "nigger" meant, but I knew they were not supposed to call me that word. I happened to be carrying a pink-and-white checkered tin lunch box, and I had placed a few of my books from class inside. Before I knew it, I swung the lunch box and hit one of the girls in the head. I knocked her out cold and dared the other girls to try me. The teachers and staff came running. I was taken to the principal's office and told that I was going to pay dearly for my actions. I was scared to death. I thought Betty and Pop were going to be so mad that they would spank me for sure. Boy was I wrong.

When Betty walked into that office, she smiled at me and grabbed my hand. The principal advised that my behavior would not be tolerated in the school. Betty responded by cussing him out. Everyone in the office looked stunned. They could not fathom that this beautiful, well-dressed woman had the mouth of a sailor. She told the staff that she knew I would never start a fight and demanded that the little racist bitch I hit receive the same punishment as me. I did not know that they had already informed Betty and Pop that I would be expelled from school for my actions. Pop tried his best to calm Betty down. She was only making the situation worse. This behavior fed into their perception that we were subclass because we were black. I admit it felt good to know that Betty had my back and she was not going to let anyone take advantage of me. Pop negotiated a two-week suspension contingent upon my good behavior.

Visiting my mother in rehab was my salvation. I had never seen her this sober, happy, and vibrant. I could not wait for her to come home so we could be reunited for good. When she came home, she was on her grind. She quickly obtained a nine-to-five job and found an apartment a few blocks from Betty and Pop's house. She did not want me to move to a new school district. My mom and dad had a brief chance to see one another before my dad's sentencing. Their love for one another never diminished. Although they knew they would never be together again, they had an unbreakable bond. My dad even spent a few evenings with my mom, unbeknownst to Mona and James. I imagine their short time they had together was bittersweet. My mother was also pursuing a music career. A few nights during the week, we would go to a music studio in New York City so she could lay tracks and sing background for other musical artists. It was great to be reunited with my mom, just me and her against the world.

On most weekends, I was with family traveling on the three-hour bus ride to Leesburg prison in South Jersey to visit my father. Visiting him in prison was the most excruciating thing to do, especially when it came to saying goodbye. I tried hard to hide my tears, but I missed him terribly.

Meanwhile, James was eager to move in, but my mom advised that she needed to put me and my needs first. I also believe she needed time to reconcile her feelings for my father. James stayed over on the weekends. Whenever my mom was around, he was nice as can be. When my mom left the room or ran out of the house to run an errand, his demeanor toward me changed. He would order me to wait on him and call me spoiled. He would say things like, "When I move in here for good, things are going to change." Although I was happy to be with my mother, I was also guarded.

I have always been observant; it is one of my gifts. I knew that this man had two very different sides to him. I was afraid to tell my mother. She seemed to be so happy. I did not want to be the reason for any discord in their relationship, so I kept quiet. I found solace in playing with the neighborhood kids. One day I was outside jumping rope with a few friends on the block. One of the little girls, a notorious bully, punched me in the nose. I was an easy target because she knew I was afraid of her.

Adam brought me home with a bloodied nose. My mother asked me if I hit the girl back. I said, "No, Mommy, I did not want to fight her." My mother walked into the bedroom and grabbed a belt and said to me, "If you don't go out there and whoop that girl's ass, I'm going to wear you out with this belt!" She grabbed me by the arm and marched me outside, Adam by my side. When we approached the kids, they were laughing. My mother asked which girl hit me. I pointed her out, and my mom said, "You know what to do."

Before I knew it, I let out all my rage and had beaten the girl up. She was crying. I could not believe it. I was terrified of the girl, and in the end my fear had been unwarranted. She was not the big and bad bully she portrayed herself to be. As an adult, I realize that my mom's reaction for me to respond with violence may not have been the best way to handle the situation. However, it did teach me how to stand up for myself.

James began to come over more frequently, and I began to act out. I ran away and went missing for hours. I didn't run far. I was right in the neighborhood at Adam's house.

He and his older brother agreed to hide me until I was ready to go home. Adam's parents eventually realized I was in the house and called my grandparents to come and get me. My mom was livid and relieved at the same time. She hugged me so tight, then yelled at me for scaring her and the family so badly. I did not realize it then, but I was starving for attention. I was rebelling against her relationship with James. I felt bad about myself because I knew James would not be good for my mother, yet I was helpless. Unbeknownst to me, James used my behavior to justify why a "father figure" was needed in the household. My mom eventually gave in. ■

## Dear Reader,

here are two life-affirming lessons that I want to share from this chapter. The first is about Love, a crazy, heart-consuming emotion that sometimes makes you do foolish things. Your love of self and the higher power you serve must supersede your love of anyone else, including your spouse and children. It's not selfish. It's necessary to keep your sanity and to keep you grounded. My grandfather compromised his morals and was willing to sacrifice his career and freedom to prevent my father from facing the consequences of his actions. Bailing your loved ones out so they don't have to face consequences hinders them from the preparation required to learn and grow from their mistakes. It also puts an unnecessary burden on you to serve a role as their savior. Sometimes the greatest gift of love you can give is to let go and pray that your loved ones have the strength and courage to figure it out for themselves. My grandfather's good intentions to protect my dad resulted in a son who was always codependent on others and unable to stand tall in his manhood.

The second lesson is about bullies. The sheer fact is they are people who lack self-confidence. They secretly yearn for power to make them feel good about themselves. When you come across people who behave in an intimidating and bullish way, take the time to respond as opposed to reacting. Be smart in how you demonstrate that you cannot be intimidated by their words and actions. Words have power and are truly mightier than the sword. I once had a manager who told me that no one in the company thought I was talented. I could have reacted with anger or feeling defeated. However, here was the reality: This person was leaving the company with minimal years of service because they could not cut it. I responded by *advising my manager that I was celebrating fourteen years of a stellar career and service. I hugged this person and wished them well with a big smile on my face. I can tell you, it was a mind-blowing experience for the bully. My response did not let this person obtain the power they were seeking, evidenced by the tears and this person's quick exit from my office. This was validation that I indeed held the power. It's simply mind over matter.*

*Warm regards,*

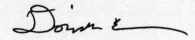

## CHAPTER 6

# Devil in Disguise

MY MOM DECIDED TO move in with James when I finished second grade. We moved into an apartment complex in East Orange. I went back to my old school, Ashland. This was not a hard transition for me because I had attended the school in kindergarten and first grade. I still had many friends there. The first few months were good. Mom went to work and to the recording studio on the weekends. James looked for employment during the day. He would walk me to school in the mornings. I remember walking down the street with him and women staring and whistling at him. He was stunningly handsome and tall, with caramel-brown skin, deep brown eyes, and a bright smile. He was well-dressed too.

I do not ever remember James working. He was always home in the mornings and after school. I never discussed his working situation with my mom, but I knew that his lack of employment took a toll on her. She was not the type of woman who would willingly take care of a grown man. He was a dreamer. He sold her lots of stories about what he would do for us once he was on his feet. But he lacked the drive to put in the work to accomplish his dreams.

In 1979, Donna Summer was killing the music charts. I remember my mom and I jamming to "Bad Girls" and

"Hot Stuff." Michael Jackson's *Off the Wall* album was in regular rotation in our house. One weekend, my mom, Nicky, and I hung out in New York. I remember Mom playing around as we walked down the street. She began to sing a rendition of Prince's "I Wanna Be Your Lover," and people started gathering around to listen. Before we knew it, she had commanded a crowd with her angelic voice and energetic spirit. She was magnetic! It was the first time we heard "Rapper's Delight" by the Sugar Hill Gang. Someone blasted the song on the beatbox, and we were all enamored with this new rap music. My mom kept listening, and before I knew it, she had memorized the lyrics and she and Nicky had their own private performance with me on the train ride home. They were horrible rappers, but we had fun pretending.

That evening when Mom and I returned home, James was waiting. He was sitting on the couch in the dark. In an instant, my mom and I realized he was angry. He literally looked like the devil; his eyes were red and glossy. He began yelling at my mother, "Where the fuck have you been?" My mother was a spitfire, so she was not intimidated by his tone. She advised that she had been out having a good time with her daughter and Nicky. She told him to get off his ass, get sober, and find a job instead of worrying about what she was doing all the time. She grabbed my hand, and we began walking toward my bedroom.

Before we hit the door, he grabbed my mother by the back of her neck and began beating her like she was a punching bag. I jumped in and tried my best to stop him, yelling and crying, "Please stop hitting my mother!" I was no match for a grown man. He threw me across the floor.

My mother yelled, "Nooo! Don't put your hands on her."

She demanded I go to my room. I did not want to leave her. She was bleeding. Her eyes were puffy, and I could tell she was in a lot of pain. She said, "Go to your room, baby. I'll be alright."

I did as my mother said and went in my room. Then I heard her say to James, "Don't you ever put your hands on my daughter."

He responded with, "Shut up, bitch!" I heard scuffling from him dragging her into their bedroom. A few hours later, I was jarred awake by a presence in my room. James was standing with a belt in his hand. He told me I better keep my mouth shut or he would beat my ass. Before I could respond, he walked out. The next morning the house was quiet. James cooked breakfast. He was singing and acting like what had happened the evening before was insignificant. He was giving my mother ice packs to put on her face and bruised body. He kept stating how sorry he was and that it would never happen again. I knew it was a lie, but I stayed silent. For sure, my mother did not believe this bullshit. Then he told her he had something that would make her feel better and told me to go to my room to watch television. I now know that "feel better" equated to heroin.

In the weeks and months that passed, I saw a dramatic shift in my mother. She started nodding again at night. She was no longer at peace. The joy in her spirit had diminished. I have never understood why she was unable to disconnect from James. When you allow others to control your emotions, you are allowing them to steal your joy. If you have people in your life who create nothing but noise and chaos, you will never have peace. You have to let them go for your own mental well-being.

I focused on my schoolwork. I hated being home. My mom worked at a law firm and sometimes worked late. James picked me up from school on most days. To impress the other parents, he would greet me as if he were happy to see me. He was a damn trip! His ability to flip the switch into different characters was amazing. He should have been an actor. This man was terrorizing me mentally. His true spirit was filled with devilish behavior. I was the only one who knew he really hated me. He spanked me with a belt every day when we arrived home. He was careful to hit my buttocks, legs, and back, so my mother would not see the whips. I did not tell my mother he was beating me for fear she would react and he would kill her. You see, he told me if I said anything, he would snap her neck. He knew how to control me. He was beating my mom at night at least three times a week. I had no reason to disbelieve him. I would lie in my bed listening to him yell and hit my mother. All I could do was hope that he would not come into my bedroom to beat me next. All too often, after he doped up my mom, he would come in my room and swing the belt. I became immune to the beatings. I began thinking about all the ways I could kill him. My spirit was engulfed with rage.

My mom befriended a neighbor who lived on the floor below our apartment. She had three children who were a few years older than me—twin girls named Lola and Pam and their older brother, Jason. They were all very popular teenagers with lots of friends. They were quick to befriend me and treated me as if I were their younger sister. They were my salvation. One evening, Mom and I were in their apartment watching *The Exorcist*. I remember being really scared but holding it in so I would not be perceived as a baby. I fell asleep, and when Pam attempted to take off my shirt to put on my nightgown she saw my bruises. She was visibly shaken and ran to get her mom and my mother. They asked what had happened to me and how I got the bruises on my back. My mother knew instantly. I told them James beat me every day after school. My mother began to cry. They knew he was abusing my mother; they could hear the fighting and arguing through the walls. No one knew until then that he was beating me too.

My mother and I slept at their apartment that night. Mom called Molly and told her that she needed to get away from James. Molly came in an instant. She walked with my mom and me into the apartment so we could gather our things. James was waiting, and Molly was ready. She told him not to think about putting his hands on us. James realized he had been exposed. Molly called him all kinds of names. He told Molly that he loved my mother and me, and he wanted to work things out. Molly advised him to go straight to hell. We gathered our things as Molly stood guard in the living room watching James on the couch.

We left and stayed with Molly for a few weeks. We ended up back at the apartment with James. Somehow, he convinced my mother to return. This time, my mom arranged for Lola and Pam to pick me up after school. Mom bought me a dog named Sheba. She was a German Shepherd and Husky mix. Sheba did not like James and did not let him near me. Whenever James came close, Sheba would growl and show her teeth. I don't know how, but Sheba knew he was evil. She slept by my bed every night and if James attempted to enter, she would bark and growl. He feared Sheba and hated that he was no longer in control. Sheba was my gift from God. I had a few months of peace before the devil figured out a way to destroy it.

At this point I was not afraid to be in the apartment with James alone. I knew if he attempted to hit me, Sheba would bite his hand off. I looked forward to coming home and playing with my beloved dog. When I was in the fifth grade, I came home from school one day and knew something was odd. Sheba did not greet me at the door. As I walked toward the bedroom, James walked up behind me. He advised that he rode Sheba down the parkway and dropped her off. He told me she probably got run over by a car and died. Then he punched me in the back and as I fell to the ground, he kicked me in my stomach. I didn't cry. I was so angry, I wanted to kill him. In that moment, I believed I was capable of murder. There was a rage inside of me that I could no longer contain. He walked away with a grin. He thought he was in control. Little did he know, I was no longer afraid of him. When my mother came home, they had a big argument about Sheba. I told my mother I hated James and I was going to tell Pop what he was doing to us. In my mind, I could imagine Pop shooting him. I wanted James to die. My mother asked me not to tell Pop or any of the Joneses. At the time, I thought she wanted to protect James. But I found out later that she was afraid they would take me for good and we would be separated.

Mom arranged for me to stay at my friend's house after school. She and her mom lived two blocks away. It worked for a few weeks, then one day James decided to pick me up from school. He told my friend's mom that my mother asked him to pick me up because we had plans. I knew he was lying. He had a black bag in his hand. When we walked up a few blocks, he pulled an extension cord from the bag and began beating me as we walked up the street. No one stopped him, but someone told my Uncle Buck. You see, everyone knew I was related to the "Jones" and my uncles were very well-known in the neighborhood.

When my mother came home, she told James he had to go. He had the audacity to tell my mother that he hated me because she always put her love for me first. He finally admitted what I already knew: He literally hated me. My mother advised him that I would always be first in her life. Before she could blink, James threw her across the room. I ran into the kitchen and grabbed a cast-iron frying pan. I was no longer going to allow this man to abuse me or my mother. When he saw me swinging the pan, he became enraged. "You little bitch. You gonna hit me with that pan?"

I demanded he stay away from my mother. Mom got up off the floor and attempted to diffuse the situation. James was so angry, he hit her and threw her across the room. I could see her struggling to get to me. She knew even with the frying pan, I was no match for James. It was too late. James snatched the pan out of my hand. I saw the terror in my mom's eyes as she struggled to save me. I fell to my knees and had my hands and arms over my head trying to protect myself from the blow of the pan. You see, James held the pan over his head, and it was clear he was going to hit me with it. I was about to die. But God had another plan.

It was by his grace and mercy that Lola, Pam, and Jason heard the commotion coming from our apartment. Jason kicked the door in, and Lola and Pam arrived just in time to grab the pan out of James's hand. They surrounded James and told him that they would beat his ass if he ever put his hands on me again. They were teenagers, respected for their clout, and they were known to be good fighters. James knew they would beat his punk ass if provoked; they were a wild bunch. They brought my mother and me downstairs to their apartment.

Pop advised my mother that he was coming to get me. Uncle Buck had told him what had happened, and he was not having any of it. He also informed my mother that they were going to kill James when they saw him. My mother called James's parents to advise them that he was in big trouble and they needed to come and get him. I think my mother was relieved. Pop picked me up and asked me why I never told him that James was beating us. He swore to me that he would kill him if he ever caught up with him. My dad called collect from prison that evening, and I told him everything. I knew he was heartbroken. He was helpless and unable to protect me. That had to make him feel terrible. He was worried about my mother. He did not understand how she allowed this to happen. That weekend when I visited him in prison, he gave me a long lecture, advising me never to let anyone put their hands on me again. My dad boxed in prison. He told me the secret to knocking someone out: Hit the person under the chin as hard as you can and follow up with a blow to the temple. The only way he could protect me was to teach me what he knew. Unfortunately, teaching a child full of rage how to fight was not a good idea.

My mother did not want to be separated from me. She arranged to obtain another apartment in the same complex. She swore that she and James were through. I went back home, and things were good. Nicky was at our apartment all the time, and we had lots of fun. I knew my mother and Nicky were getting high, but I had no qualms about it. My mom went to work and took care of me, and James was no longer living with us. Life was much better. Unfortunately, James conned his way back into our lives. He was obsessed with my mother. He did not move in, but he visited often. My mother refused to give him keys to the apartment and did not want him around me at all. I stayed with Nicky or my grandparents whenever he visited. The mere thought of James made me sick.

I was now in seventh grade and my grades and good behavior started to plummet because James was visiting more often. I was popular in school and had a lot of friends. I did not start fights, but I seemed to always be in them. I did not like to argue. If someone attempted to argue with me, I responded by punching them in the face. I was out of control. I remember beating this girl's head on the curb and getting excited by the sight of her blood on the ground.

As I reflect on that time, I thank God that someone broke up the fight. I could have killed her, and I know I was capable of it. I was full of rage. I recently ran into a girl, now a full-grown woman, I had beat in the head with my high-heel shoe in the cafeteria. I approached her to apologize and realized that she now suffered from schizophrenia. She was afraid of me and began spinning in circles, screaming. I never told my family about the incident. I felt horrible. I wanted her to know that I was no longer the violent girl she knew in school. I am free of the hopelessness, depression, and anger that raged inside me for so long. Unfortunately, I cannot go back and change the past. Therefore, I cannot dwell on the things I am unable to change. I can only move forward and try my best to repent by utilizing my gifts and talents to serve and give back to others.

Now I'm going to fast-forward to the end of the school year. All my friends were excited about moving on to the eighth grade. I had a boyfriend and lost my virginity to him. He was a super-nice kid who was a few years older than me. I liked him a lot, and he allowed me to release some of the anger and depression I was feeling. I received straight F's the entire school year. It wasn't that I could not do the work; I simply had no interest. My teacher told me I was a loser who would repeat seventh grade. She was an asshole. If that was her attempt to make me change my behavior, she had gone about it all wrong. How about asking why a girl in the gifted and talented program and a former honor roll student suddenly stopped caring? I was called into the principal's office a few weeks before school ended. My mom and Molly were sitting in the office. The principal informed us that I scored in the top tenth percentile on the national standardized test. He advised that they had no choice but to promote me to eighth grade. God had interceded again.

It was the beginning of summer, and I had spent the whole day at the park with my boyfriend and some friends. When I came home, James was sitting on the couch, naked and high as a kite. He ordered me to, "Come here." I ran out and fled to Lola and Pam's house. I called Pop, screaming for him to pick me up. I was told Uncle Buck had gone back to my mother's apartment to kill James, but he wasn't there. When I told my mother what happened, she called me a liar. I could not believe it. It was like someone had sucker punched me. I couldn't help but ask myself, who is this woman and where is my mother?

My mother knew that once the Jones family got wind of this, James's days were numbered, so she made sure he stayed with his family in Plainfield. This also provided her the opportunity to escape the abuse. She packed her things and moved with her parents for a few months. I refused to go back to her. My dad was coming home soon, and I needed a break from the madness of James and my mother, a woman I barely recognized anymore. Not long after Mom left James, he began to stalk her. He showed up outside of her job and threw gasoline on her to set her on fire. Her coworkers jumped him before he could light the match. James was arrested, and that was the last I ever heard or saw of him. I don't know or care about his whereabouts. ∎

# Dear Reader,

hen God puts a vision in your head, it is up to you to put in the work with fortitude to make it happen. James was unwilling to put in the work, which led to frustration and an unhealthy codependence on my mother. When you make someone else your everything, you are depriving yourself of control. You are unable to experience the personal fulfillment you can achieve from your own essence. Codependence is your way of telling the world that you are not good enough. You can't stand on your own. It's a dysfunction of your inability to love yourself.

It took me leaving for my mom to wake up. You see, her love for me was never in doubt. It was the lack of love for herself that led to her despair. I vowed from this experience never to be a victim. I would never let anyone put their hands on me or bully me again. My cousins gave me the nickname "Duke" because I was a fighter. Being away from the chaos allowed me to channel my anger. Because at one point the anger controlled me and brought out the worst in me. I did not like that person when I looked in the mirror. I still have the fight in me, but I use it wisely without violence. My fight provided me the courage to stand up and have a voice. We are all born with a voice, and your voice matters. Don't play yourself small by hiding your voice inside. My voice enabled me to champion for women and underserved communities of color and create my own job within a Fortune 100 company.

*I am now advocating for victims of domestic violence and for viable solutions for drug addicts and their children. How are you channeling your anger? How are you using your voice?*

*Warm regards,*

# CHAPTER 7

# The Calm before the Storm

WHILE LIVING WITH POP and Betty, I started the eighth grade at a new school on the other side of town. I was placed in the gifted and talented class and my grades got back on track. Although we were a class full of bright kids, we were very mischievous. We blew up the science teacher's desk. We snuck into the vice principal's office, stole his vodka, and poured it into the grape juice fountain during lunch. There were a handful of us who frequented the principal's office to get the paddle across our backsides for our bad behavior. We didn't care. We received good grades and took pride in enjoying our adolescence. I was caught up in the fun of middle school. I immediately made great friends and looked forward to going to school each day.

Meanwhile, my father got released from prison that fall and life was good. He moved in with Mona and Shane in the Orange Projects. He frequented Betty and Pop's house daily to ensure he spent time with me and the family. His first big gesture was to ensure that I was the flyest girl in the annual school fashion show. He called Aunt Mary and Barron's old girlfriend, one of the best boosters on the East Coast. They came over to Betty's house with a whole wardrobe of clothes for me to choose from. I chose a leather outfit, a stylish dress, and a low-cut bathing suit. Aunt

Ethel lent me her fox fur coat, and Aunt Mary made me practice walking.

I'll never forget that fashion show. I rocked that stage like I owned it. For my final walk, I wore the fur coat that covered the bathing suit I had on underneath with a big straw black hat and high heels. I walked across the stage and then dropped the fur coat to the floor, dragging it as I strutted across the runway. The crowd went wild with cheer. Mary was front and center cheering me on, "You go, girl!" Betty and Ethel were right beside her. My dad sat in the front row, grinning. I could see from the stage that he had quite a few women admirers looking his way. When he returned from prison, he had a noticeably buff physique. I could tell he had worked out in the gym during his incarceration.

The school was literally a block away from Pop and Betty's house, so we walked home after the fashion show. I remember Ethel teasing me about dragging her fur coat. "Did you lose your mind dragging my damn coat? Bitch, you act like you Diana Ross or some goddamn body!" Aunt Mary chimed in, "Say what you want to say, she was the baddest chick on that stage, Ethel." The Jones sisters laughed as they continued their usual banter. Whenever the three sisters were together, you were guaranteed to witness a playful exchange of teasing remarks.

Pop helped my dad secure a job as a barber to earn income. His continued heroin use was obvious. He no longer used needles to ingest the drug. Betty and Pop lived in a three-family home, owned by Uncle Buck's girl-friend. They occupied the first floor. There were tenants on the second floor, and the third floor was empty. Mimi and I would sometimes sneak our friends to the third floor. There was one instance when I snuck up the stairs only to be shocked by walking in on Uncle Buck in the act of shooting up. I thought for sure he would be pissed; at the very least, embarrassed. He was not. He said very calmly to me, "You see this right here?" as he continued to shoot heroin into his arm. "This is a demon I would not wish on my worst enemy. Don't ever use drugs. They will destroy you. Do you hear me?" I nodded to gesture yes. "Now get your ass back to school before I tell Betty you were up here." I never mentioned the incident, and neither did he.

I spent the weekends with my father and Mona in the projects. Unbeknownst to me, Isaiah's kids lived in the neighborhood. My dad, ridden with guilt, would give them a few dollars on occasion to buy snacks from the store. Apparently, a relative found out and was not happy. One day, two young men approached my dad and me as we were walking from the store to our apartment. They exchanged words with my dad and attempted to jump him. I remember Dad telling me to run and tell Mona what was going on. I didn't listen to him. There was no freaking way I was leaving my father to fight two men without jumping in. My dad really didn't need my help. Those two young men were not prepared. A few jabs, and they were both on the ground looking stupid.

A crowd had gathered and there were a few people laughing. Someone said, "That's what happens when you fuck with an OG. These young boys ain't ready. Much respect, Bubu." My dad nodded and grabbed my hand, and we walked quickly to our apartment. I remember him saying, "Damn, I don't need this shit! If my parole officer finds out, I'm screwed." Then he turned his head and looked me dead in my eyes. "And so you think you Rocky now. I told you to run. What if they had guns?"

I replied, "Then we would have died together. I wasn't scared."

My dad responded, shaking his head in disbelief, "That's the damn problem. You ain't scared of nothing." My dad was not a disciplinarian. He let me stay out without a curfew. The truth is that I was not one to follow rules. I was so hardheaded, he would have been forced to discipline me. I did not realize it then, but now as I look back, I believe the guilt and regrets he held related to my childhood and his inability to parent weighed heavily on his heart.

As the months passed, my dad's weight loss became noticeable. In less than one year after his release, he was diagnosed with AIDS. To cope with this death sentence, Dad coupled alcoholism with his heroin use. Rum was his drink of choice. He was always a quiet and reserved man. When he drank alcohol, he spoke his truth. Although I would never condone the use of alcohol to find your courage, it was so refreshing to see him speak up for himself and tell people how he really felt instead of burying his feelings. He finally had the courage to do so. Betty was known to cuss Pop out on a regular basis for the most insignificant things. It made us all very uncomfortable. I remember my dad telling Betty that she needed to stop being so hard on Pop. He told her to let go of baggage from years ago and holding Pop hostage for his past mistakes. I did not know what he meant at the time, but Betty would come to confide her secrets to me when I became a woman.

My grandmother Betty was a force to be reckoned with. I remember being arrested for fighting. I was fifteen and jumped by two grown women ages nineteen and twenty-six over a local drug dealer I was messing around with, but wasn't really feeling, for a long-term love affair. I for sure would not fight over him if I had the choice. The women were totally in the wrong for fighting a minor. But when the police arrived, it appeared that I was the aggressor given that I was getting the best of both women. So, they arrested all of us. Betty and Ethel arrived at the police station shortly after and raised all kind of hell. Betty demanded that the detective release me immediately. The detective had hands the size of a small basketball with visible track marks from using drugs. Betty knew he was an addict; he was Pop's former partner.

Betty screamed at him, "You junkie muthafucka, you let my granddaughter go right now or I'll burn this muthafucka down."

He responded by pulling his glasses closer to the tip of his nose, tilting his head, looking her in the eyes, and asking, "Do I need to call Pop?"

She began to let off all kinds of expletives. In the meantime, the two women and I were chained to the bench, bloody and battered. Ethel approached the two women and asked, "Did you two punk bitches jump my niece?" Before they could get the words out of their mouths, Ethel slapped them in their faces, and then just like that it was all-out mayhem in the police station. As a result, we were all chained to the benches on opposites sides of the room. My grandfather appeared out of nowhere with his usual grin, shaking his head, and we were miraculously released, leaving the two women behind.

My father called Mona and a few of my cousins to confront the women. We went to Munn Avenue where the two women were known to live and frequent. My father demanded that both women shoot me a fair one. One of the women jumped in my dad's face and before I knew it, Mona had the woman in a headlock, dragging her in the street. The next thing I knew, there was a total of twenty to thirty people fighting in the street. As soon as we all heard the police sirens, we scattered from the scene. We returned to Betty and Pop's house and spent the evening reminiscing about the day's escapades.

When the dust settled from our fight, I was punished by being expelled from East Orange High School. I subsequently moved in with Molly and my mother on the other side of town to attend Scott High School. Molly had a one-bedroom apartment. It was a tight squeeze for the three of us to share the space, but we made it work. My dad's health began to decline fast, and Betty started telling everyone that he had cancer. My father told me the real deal from the beginning, and I knew he felt shamed by his AIDS diagnosis.

School was my social space. I had little regard for my grades. Most of the work came easy, so I skated by without studying. I had no trouble attracting the opposite sex, and as a result, I was a very promiscuous teenager, longing for a loving and committed relationship. I was attracted to older men; the boys my age were way too immature and did not stimulate me intellectually.

During this time, I met Tammy. She was stunningly beautiful with a big personality and infectious smile. We saw one another in the halls, but we did not have any mutual friends. She lived in Newark. We officially met on the bus. She was in the back cutting up, cracking on some of the boys who vied for her attention. She immediately befriended me. I remember her saying, "Yo, shorty, why you so quiet? Come back here and school these boys on why they could never have women like me and you."

I remember being enamored by her boldness. She said the things I was thinking but would never say out loud. Tammy was a breath of fresh air, the friend I needed to get me through that season of my life. We were "ride or die" for one another. I loved her like a sister. She saw a sadness in me, and me in her, that only the two of us could understand. We were both victims of abuse as children—her, molestation, and me, domestic violence. When I decided to drop out of high school, she and her mom took me in. Tammy's mother was sweet, but Tammy clearly ran the show in the household. Her mom worked the graveyard shift. We were two promiscuous teenagers on our own living our lives with no boundaries or cares.

We hit the clubs frequently and only dated drug dealers with money. Although we were both quite capable of taking care of ourselves, we saw no need to work when we had multiple admirers willing to give us money to showcase us as their trophy pieces. We had to be kept to a certain standard, designer bags and clothes, wining and dining. We had the mentality that money talked and bullshit walked. We were so shallow in our thinking. I remember this guy who went out of his way to date me. He had tons of dough, but when he picked me up for a date, his attire was not up to par and I felt that I could not be seen with him. I know that I hurt his feelings. I told him he was not up to my standard and that I could not be seen with him. I slammed the door in his face. He did not deserve this treatment, but I was too immature to understand that it is the heart and soul that counts.

My dad's declining health began to send me into a tailspin. I began splitting my time between Tammy's and the projects to visit him. One day, Betty was rushed to the emergency room for chest pain. Dad and I were in the waiting room with Ethel and a few other family members. He purchased a soda from the vending machine and drank a few sips. Without regard, I picked up the can and took a few sips as well. My father yelled at me, "Put that down! Don't ever drink or eat after me. You may get sick." I remember the look of panic and fear on his face.

I looked him dead in the eye and said, "If I'm going to die because I drank after you, then so be it!"

Ethel was visibly upset by the exchange. She said to my dad, "Bubu, it's going to be alright. She ain't gonna get sick drinking after you. She loves you. We all love you. Don't be so hard on yourself."

The silence was deafening. My dad just nodded and we all sat quietly waiting for Pop to tell us the status of Betty's condition. In the mid-1980s there were still a lot of unknowns and false information circulating about how the AIDS virus was contracted. When my father was diagnosed, Betty purchased paper products so my dad would not eat off the plates and silverware. I'm sure she did not mean to make him feel ashamed, but he was. He knew there was a fear that we could somehow catch the virus by his mere presence. My dad did not understand that he could not control the circumstances life threw at him. To wallow in shame was not going to change the outcome. All we can do in these situations is accept the hand we've been given, stay positive, and love one another.

Betty had been diagnosed with cirrhosis of the liver years earlier when we lived in Irvington. The doctor told her if she took one more drink, she would die. The thought of death and her own mortality had provided her the courage to quit cold turkey. She never looked back. There's a quote that says, "Strength doesn't come from what you can do. It comes from overcoming the things you thought you could not do." Betty's ability to overcome her addiction showed me the strength of her soul and spirit. I'm sure she was tempted, but she conquered that alcohol demon head-on and beat it down. She subsequently suffered from high blood pressure and heart disease, controlled by medication.

Living in the projects, I was offered to earn money by being a mule for some of the dope dealers, but that did not interest me. I wasn't stupid enough to risk jail time for small change. I also had no desire to stand on the corner and run drugs for someone else either. Most of the kids who stood on the corners were desperate to survive. That made it easy for the drug distributor to find workers. Many of the parents were strung out on crack. I remember this one family—the mother was single and had six children. She was known as hardworking and a good provider for her children. When she became addicted to crack, she neglected and abandoned her children on a regular basis. Right before Thanksgiving, her son knocked on our door to advise my dad that his mom had stolen their turkey and sold it. My father and I took him to the store and bought the family groceries. My father told him not to let his mother in their home if she came back. I remember thinking how sad and embarrassing it was for those children. Everyone knew their mom was a crack fiend and would do anything to get high. To steal food from your children's mouths was a low blow. Little did I know my own mother would succumb to the addiction of crack.

Who was I to judge their circumstance? Did my judgment define them or me? At that point in time, it defined me. Who was I to judge their mother's addiction, knowing that my parents were suffering from the same disease. Were my parents any better than their mother? The answer is no. They were all children of God, struggling with the disease of addiction.

My dad began to complain that he was in pain all the time. Some days he forced himself to get out of bed. The only thing that kept him functioning was heroin. At this point, he was barely working and unable to pay for his drug habit. I began dating the son of a major drug dealer who had recently been sent to federal prison. His dad was also a good friend of my cousin Barron. This young man, named Harry, was enamored with his father's lifestyle, but he was no bona fide street hustler. He was educated, went to the best prep school in the county, and was a truly nice guy. I immediately recognized he had no game. He fell for me way too fast and way too easy. He began to brag about a huge shipment of marijuana coming in from overseas worth $60,000 in street value.

Without hesitation, I immediately began planning how to beat him out of his stash. One of my dear friends in the projects, Terrance, happened to be one of the biggest drug dealers in the area. He was dating Tammy at the time. He was a fly dresser and always looked out for me. He would let me drive his car with no license and often treated Tammy and me to shopping sprees. He was my dude, and I loved and trusted him like a brother. I told Terrance what was up. I introduced him to Harry. Terrance told Harry that he wanted to buy the shipment. Harry knew Terrance was a legit dealer, so it never dawned on him that we were setting him up. We convinced Harry to deliver the marijuana to my Moana's apartment. Once he verified the shipment was good, Terrance would pay him $25,000. Harry agreed, and Terrance gave him a $5,000 down payment in good faith. Harry was so excited. I could tell this was his first major deal. He took me out to dinner that evening and could not stop talking about how cool Terrance had been.

A few days later, as promised, Harry and two other young men pulled up to the projects in a minivan. Terrance had paid one of his runners, a low-level drug dealer named Squeak, $1,000 to rob Harry when he arrived. Squeak and two other men rolled up on Harry and his friends with guns blazing and stole the drugs. Harry was mortified and scared. He ran to my dad's apartment in a panic. I acted surprised and paged Terrance. He called a few minutes later and advised Harry that he would try to find out who stole his

supply. Terrance also advised that Harry now had a problem, because he needed to deliver or return the $5,000 he
had been given as a deposit. Harry was visibly upset, yet
he and his friends were talking gangster about what they
were going to do to the robbers. It was all game, street rule
101: If you are making a major drug deal, you carry a gun.
Neither he nor his two friends were packing. They were easy
and gullible targets.

My father knew I had introduced Terrance to Harry, but
he had no idea that we had set up the robbery. He sent
Harry and his friends home, then lectured me about
getting in the middle of a drug deal. He knew his lecture
was going in one ear and out the other. I paid him no mind.
Terrance and I met up at Tammy's house that evening and
discussed how we were going to package the marijuana
for quick distribution and sale. Within a week, we sold the
entire stash in bulk and split the profit fifty/fifty. I now had
enough to buy a kilo of cocaine. Terrance took me under
his wing to ensure I was protected. He managed the day
to day with the runners. I managed the business, packag-
ing, and payments. Terrance had an apartment around
the corner from Tammy, so it was easy for me to meet up
with him. I did not want Tammy involved with any of this,
so we never conducted business at her house. Terrance
and I acquired more runners, totaling fifteen people who
were actively selling our product. I was rolling in dough
quickly. Harry realized that he had been duped when I
disappeared. He did not know Tammy or where she lived,
so I stayed there while Terrance managed drug flow in
the projects. A few weeks later, my dad came to Tammy's
house in a panic. "Dorinda, they are going to kill you! What
the fuck is wrong with you. Are you crazy? Harry may be
a punk kid, but his father is not. He cannot let this live.
He has to retaliate." I could sense the fear in my father's

voice. But I had already thought the possibility of retaliation through. I knew that if Barron found out my life was in danger, he would intercede. Harry's father was in prison, and although he could order the hit, he could not guarantee Barron would not retaliate by killing his family. Everyone knew that Barron would protect his family at all costs. I was banking on it. Sure enough, my dad called Barron to tell him what was up. Barron advised he would take care of it. I don't know the details, but I know that a few days later, Barron advised my father I was safe. Barron also made a point of lecturing me. I nodded and agreed to whatever he was saying out of respect.

I began supplying my parents and extended family with drugs and money. Although I did not live with my mom, we remained close and saw each other at least four times a week. Neither of my parents were happy with the situation, but they accepted it. In my mind, my dad no longer had to worry about money to supply his habit. If heroin kept him well, I would ensure he had it. My dad was my everything. I was willing to sacrifice my integrity, morals, and soul to keep him alive. I now realize I had no control over his fate. It was selfish of me to want him to wallow in his suffering here on earth. I failed to realize that I was worth so much more. Designer clothes and flashy material things did not make me happy. Girls envied me because of my outward appearance but had no idea I was a miserable soul with no self-esteem. I gave myself freely to men who were not worthy and used me like a ragdoll. I literally hated drugs because of what they did to my family, but sold them to others. I was now part of the vicious cycle that I despised. ■

# Dear Reader,

etty's inability to let go of her grudges against Pop became a heavy and unnecessary burden not only for her, but for our entire family. People who hold grudges desire to stand in their righteousness as a victim. They seek empathy and acknowledgment that they were wronged. They are unknowingly giving their power away, because they require others to validate their feelings. This ultimately leads to feelings of bitterness and resentment that will ultimately prevent a true healing. My advice to anyone holding on to a grudge is to LET IT GO! That weight you are carrying is preventing you from obtaining the inner peace you deserve. It is an unnecessary weight your heart does not have to bare. People are flawed; they make mistakes. How you cope with disappointment is totally up to you. You cannot blame people for your inability to reconcile, forgive, and move on. I refuse to hold grudges because I never want to relinquish my power to others. I won't willingly be anyone's victim again.

Looking back on the day we had the big fight, I regret that we chose physical violence as our attempt to resolve the problem. I realize that we put everyone in danger. One wrong hit, slip, or fall, and someone could have lost their life, and over what? My lack of serious feelings for a young man who clearly had no serious affection for me or the other woman he was dating. The woman I am today knows this for sure: If he's your man, he would never put you in a predicament to fight for his love. In my twenty-four years of marriage, I have never had a woman call, confront, or insinuate that my husband was unfaithful to me. I find solace in knowing that my husband is truly mine and I am his, heart, body, and soul. We both know that infidelity is a deal breaker for our marriage. We discussed and agreed to that term before we took our vows. I believe that my husband was my gift from God; his patience, love, and respect were required for my spiritual healing. My husband protects my heart at all costs.

I would also like to discuss judgment. It's a mechanism that people use to cope to feel better about the shortcomings in their own lives. We hide behind our judgment to give the false appearance that we are better than others. Who are we to value someone else less or place labels on their experience? Be careful with those feelings of judgment that provide you a false sense of superiority. I can assure you that living this life will surely bring you back to reality. You are no better than those you choose to judge. We are all God's children.

The woman I am today would never sacrifice her integrity for monetary reward. When you have integrity, you learn to do the right thing regardless of the consequence or inconvenience. I had no faith nor patience. I was arrogant enough to believe that I had control over my father's destiny. I was not willing to wait or sacrifice for material things that ultimately had no value in my life. Most of all, I was not willing to wait for my blessings. I have learned that patience is a key element of success. We live in a society of immediate gratification that tends to put us on the wrong path. Every successful person that we know has had to practice patience as part of the journey to achieving success. Steve Harvey and Tyler Perry were both homeless in pursuing their dreams. Bill Gates's first business was a complete failure. So, how did they ultimately achieve success? I can tell you for sure that their willingness to be patient and sacrifice was a key component to their success. They stayed focused and put in the hard work to pursue their passion and life's purpose. They also had an unwavering faith that enabled them to not only survive but overcome and achieve success beyond their wildest dreams. If you lack faith and are not willing to wait, sacrifice, and work hard, you will never achieve the level of success you are destined to achieve. When you lack patience, you will never *receive God's true reward for your life. Nothing worth having will come easy. Accept it and put in the work with fortitude and focus.*

*Warm regards,*

# CHAPTER 8

## Heaven Is for Real

HEN I WAS SIXTEEN, my dad was in and out of the hospital for various ailments related to his virus. I never visited him. Betty and some other family members criticized me heavily for being selfish. They did not realize that if I visited my dad, I would have to cope with the fact that he was dying. I could not handle that reality, so I chose not to.

Terrance introduced me to a man named Maurice. He was ten years older than me, very handsome, with light skin and curly hair. We had an immediate connection. Little did I know he was also a family friend. His best friend was my cousin Chad. We talked into the wee hours of the morning and quickly became lovers. He was also a drug dealer who was the major distributor in the Irvington area. We were together every night. At the time, I never questioned why he never took me to his apartment. I was fine with staying at the luxury hotel rooms he rented for us.

Not long afterward, Terrance was arrested and there I was left trying to deal with both the street and business side of our hustle. I fully anticipated that I would be tried by his runners. Once they realized Terrance was not around, it would be easy for them to try to take advantage of a girl. I had to make a choice: go all in or get out. At some point, I would be faced with a situation where I had to kill or be killed to survive. It was standard street code: kill or be killed. Was I capable of murder at the time? I believe so. But the thought of jail and loss of freedom was a worse fate. I confided my concerns to Maurice, and he convinced me to get out. He promised to take care of me and hold Terrance down. He had a generous and loving spirit, so I knew he would.

One late morning on a cold winter day, we were returning from a fabulous evening in New York City and an overnight stay at the Waldorf Astoria hotel. I had taken an unopened champagne bottle, which was sitting in my bag next to my feet in the car. Maurice was smart. He did not drive flashy cars to bring attention to himself. He had a little Chevy that he rode around in during the week, so he had less of a chance to be stopped by the police. He parked the car and walked around the corner to pick up cash from his runners.

Out of nowhere this woman approached the passenger side of the car and began banging on the window. She was screaming that she was going to beat my ass for messing with her man. My initial thought, after looking the woman up and down, was that this 'hood rat could not possibly be dating Maurice. I looked down at my Gucci boots and fur coat and thought, *I'm not messing up my clothes fighting this trifling bitch.*

I cracked the window and said, "I don't know why you want to fight me. You need to go find Maurice and beat his ass. I never knew you existed until now."

The woman began to cuss and demanded that I get out of the car. Suddenly, I heard a familiar voice yelling out the second-floor window of the house across the street, "Duke, is that you? Bitch you better get away from my cousin." It turned out that my cousin Erin, Chad's sister, was visiting Maurice's girlfriend. Erin was my father's age, and she used to babysit me often as a toddler. She, too, was a heroin addict and later diagnosed with AIDS. When I saw Erin, I knew I was covered. The woman was still banging on the window, shaking and kicking the car. I became irate and did not want to take more of her crap. For sure, she could not fathom that I was scared. I took off my fur coat and threw it in the backseat. I grabbed the champagne bottle, jumped out the car, and hit the woman in the head with the bottle.

We started fighting in the middle of the street. Erin raced out of the house screaming, "Don't you fuck with my Duke, bitch!" We jumped the woman in the middle of the street as her small children watched in horror. Maurice and a few of the young men he was hanging out with attempted to break up the fight. I was so mad, I began to fight him as well. He merely ducked and backed up as he apologized profusely. He would never hit a woman. Out of nowhere my cousin Patricia arrived on the scene driving her Bentley and scooped up Erin and me before the police came.

Patricia had traits similar to Aunt Mary's and Aunt Ethel's, but she was much more polished and sophisticated. She was smart and liked the finer things in life; she had always been attracted to fast money. Her husband was a street hustler who took good care of her financially. He ran in the same circles as my cousin Barron. She adored and loved her family and treated all of us younger clan as if we were her kids. Erin, Patricia, and Chad were the children of my uncle Skip, the youngest son of Nana Jones and her husband.

Maurice waited a few days for me to calm down. He then proceeded to tell me that he was renting a nice house and wanted me to move in with him. I agreed, and life for me was good with money flowing like water. I spent most of my days shopping and visiting family. Ethel and I hung out a lot. She was busy chasing her cheating husband, Sean. My uncle was a good provider, but he was unapologetic about his blatant infidelity. Ethel knew where his girlfriends lived. She would ride by to see if she saw his car or one of his ladies. We would often go to his favorite gambling spot to pick up her spending and bill money. Ethel would cuss him out every time, but he didn't care. He was a street runner and was not going to change.

I visited their apartment often. They had one closet filled with suitcases full of money from top to bottom. I remember thinking, *Why in the hell don't they put that money in the bank? What if a fire broke out?* One day, Ethel followed my uncle's girlfriend into her driveway and demanded that she get out of the car so she could beat her ass. The woman was clearly terrified. She knew that Ethel was going to beat her up and she was likely to get jumped. What type of niece would I be if I let my aunt fight without jumping in? Looking back, I realize that we were so freaking dysfunctional. I would never encourage my children to fight. Lord, what were we thinking?

When I was older, after Aunt Ethel passed away due to a nasty bout with cancer, I asked Uncle Sean why he never invested his money or purchased property. He said, "Baby, Ethel would have burnt down every house I had. She was one crazy bitch! One day, I came home from being away a few days, I took a bath, and woke up in a tub full of bleach. She tried to bleach me alive. She was one crazy heifer, but I would not trade her for the world. I miss her terribly. I would cut off my left arm to have one more day with her."

Maurice was making tons of dough. We lived comfortably and quickly became complacent with our lives. The only distraction was his mother, who treated him like the bottom of her shoe, even though he lavished her with money and gifts. She would always respond with a comparison to his two brothers to belittle him. One of his brothers was a punk street thug who liked to beat women; the other a decorated military man who chose to go the straight and narrow. She despised Maurice and hated me even more. She made the mistake of inviting Patricia over to her home to discuss Maurice's new girlfriend. She failed to make the connection that I was a member of the Jones family. Maurice's mother went on to tell Patricia how she despised me and wanted to break us up. She asked Patricia to assist her in setting me up for a beatdown and robbing Maurice. Patricia grinned and told her she wanted to meet me and asked her to invite me over.

Maurice and I arrived at the house. I was shocked to see Patricia sitting on the couch. Patricia said to me, "You must be Dorinda. Nice to meet you." She asked me to sit down next to her. I played along, realizing she was up to something. Maurice stood in the doorway, looking perplexed. Patricia then proceeded to tell Maurice's mother, "This young sweet girl right here is my baby cousin, and I love her like a daughter. If you ever threaten to harm her again, I will cut your throat in your own house." She then turned to Maurice. "I don't know what kind of sick shit you got going on with your momma, but you better tell her not to fuck with this girl right here. I'll send Barron over here to light this whole block up, and you know he's itching for a reason to kill you and your brother after what went down with my Chad."

A few years earlier, Maurice's brother had set my cousin Chad up to be robbed, beaten, and left on the highway to die. When Barron found out, he was livid. Maurice pleaded with Chad and Patricia to talk Barron down. I suspected Maurice had to pay Barron a large sum of money to let it go. Barron never missed an opportunity to tell me he thought Maurice was a punk. He had no respect for him and was not fond of our relationship at all.

His brother was a scumbag. He tried to sleep with me. I had no respect for this fool and thought he was a coward. I also knew he had dated a close family friend and broken her jaw. When I refused, he threatened to beat me up and pulled a crowbar from the trunk. I remember thinking, *Is this fool trying to bully me into sleeping with him? I'll gladly take the ass whooping, but his punk ass would know he was in a fight.* I got right in his face and said, "I dare you!" Barron may have let that incident with Chad slide, but I guarantee you if you touch me, the outcome will be painful and tragic for you and yours. Go ahead. Hit me." He began to laugh as if it was all a joke to test me. I knew if I said yes, he would have gladly taken advantage of me. He had no integrity or love for his brother or me. He only loved himself.

April 9, 1988—I remember this day vividly. I treated my mother to breakfast at an IHOP restaurant. We had a great time chatting it up and laughing. I gave her a new Walkman and she began to sing her favorite song at the time, "Giving You the Best that I Got" by Anita Baker. My mother had no qualms about breaking out in song anywhere. I told her I was going to visit my dad, and she asked me to send her love and confided that she was concerned about him. She told me she called him a few days prior, and he did not sound good. Although my parents never reunited, they remained the best of friends. I walked my mom to her car. As we hugged goodbye, she slipped $100 in my hand and I placed heroin in her pocket. We both knew what we were doing was wrong, but we enabled this behavior by not acknowledging it. Maurice was waiting patiently for me in the parking lot, and we both went to visit my dad to deliver his heroin.

When we entered Pop and Betty's house, my dad was lying across the couch. He could barely move. I sat next to him on the floor while Maurice took a seat across the room.

My dad and Maurice exchanged pleasantries, and my dad began to advise me on how much he loved me. He apologized for not being a good father and for introducing my mother to drugs. He believed God was punishing him for his sins and killing Isaiah. He told Maurice to take care of me—he made him promise. He then spoke the words I was not ready to hear. He said, "I'm tired. I'm not going to make it through the week. I'm going to die." I remember the feeling of panic and fear in my heart and in the pit of my stomach.

My response was so ugly, it's something I will always regret. I responded by screaming, "You are so selfish! How can you say that? I'm bringing you drugs so you won't get sick. Why are you giving up? I hate you!" Tears rolled down his face. I could tell he did not know what to say, but in the only response he could muster, he uttered: "I'm sorry." Maurice handed my dad a few Kleenex tissues from the box on the TV table, which was also covered with prescription medications. He told me to calm down. I stormed out of the house. Maurice came out ten minutes later. My dad was admitted to the hospital the next day for the last time.

On April 11, 1988, Maurice and I drove home from New York with kilos of cocaine in the trunk. Ordinarily, he would never take me with him to pick up from his distributor. We both agreed I should never be put in a position to face jail time if stopped by the police. But this day, he insisted I ride with him. He told me he needed the company. On our way home, Maurice stopped the car in front of the hospital. He looked me in the eye and told me I needed to go visit my father. I responded by telling him I had never gone to see him before in the hospital and I wasn't going to see him now. I would visit him when he was discharged at home. I hated hospitals that much. Maurice insisted he was not moving the car until I got out and went to visit my dad.

He told me Betty and Pop were upstairs expecting me. He got out of the car and opened the passenger side so I could get out. I sat there, and he then asked me not to make a scene. He told me to stop acting like a baby and to go upstairs. He knew that would piss me off, so I did as he said very reluctantly. Maurice pulled off once he saw me walk through the door.

When I entered the hospital room, my dad was hooked to a bunch of machines. He was in a coma, and my knees buckled. I felt like my heart was ripped from my chest as I hit the floor crying hysterically. Betty and Mary lifted me up off the floor and began to console me. We all sat there waiting for the inevitable. We believe my father was holding on waiting for his sister Pumpkin to arrive, but we could not reach her. She and Mimi had gone shopping at the mall.

Around seven p.m., my dad woke up as clear as day. He turned to Betty and me and said, "Bye. Nana and Buck are here to get me." Nana Jones and her son were dead, so I knew instantly they were angels and there was a heaven. My dad closed his eyes, and the next thing I saw and heard is the heart machine sounding off and a flat line rolling across the screen. He was gone, and we were all in shock. But in *that moment,* I knew heaven was for real. I found solace in knowing that my dad was in heaven with family who loved him.

We all returned to Pop and Betty's house that evening. The family did what families do in these times: We rallied together. There was food and a sense of comfort in the home. When Mimi and Pumpkin returned there, I remember greeting Mimi at the door. She looked around and saw a house full of people. I didn't have to muster the words to tell her my dad had died. I simply looked her in the eyes, and she instinctively knew. She ran off the front porch and began to weep uncontrollably. The only thing I could do was hug her. I let her know that he tried hard to wait for her and Pumpkin to say goodbye. In that moment, we knew our lives would never be the same. Mimi and I grew up like sisters. We had our ups and downs, but we were always there for each other. She never had a relationship with her biological father, so my dad and Pop were the two men in her life who meant the most to her.

As dysfunctional as my family is, I would not trade it for anything in the world. These are the people who shaped the woman I am today. They taught me the importance of love and family. I have fond memories of my time with them. Erin, Patricia, and Pumpkin passed on after my father's death, but left a profound impact on my generation of cousins, who broke the family's curse of addiction. Erin died of AIDS, Patricia lost a battle with cancer, and Pumpkin died from a heart attack.

I know they are all smiling down on me with pride because I made it. I achieved success without succumbing to the street life. No one can take my achievements away, because I earned them honestly and with integrity. I also remain my sister's keeper by dedicating my career to empowering women to achieve success. This is something that Lily Jones instilled in her family—the importance of giving back to others. As dysfunctional as they all were, there was not one person in the Jones family who would not give a dollar to the homeless or feed and clothe those in need. They taught me to be empathetic to others and their circumstance. ■

# Dear Reader,

*O*ften, we confuse our need for validation and attention for love. Maurice's girlfriend chose to let her kids watch her act like a fool over a man who did not love or respect her. As such, the immature young woman in me had no reason to respect her or her children. Our altercation was a clear example of two women who had no standards or boundaries. We were both women who struggled with low self-esteem and self-worth, looking for a man to validate our mere existence.

It took the death of my aunt Ethel for my uncle Sean to realize he should have spent more time with his wife. Aunt Ethel never received the validation she was seeking. Uncle Sean's inability to be faithful to her as they grew older left her heartbroken. When we fail to set boundaries and expectations on how we are treated, we open the doorway and enable others to treat us badly. Whether it's a lover, family, or a business relationship, you must set standards on how people can treat you.

I once worked under a senior executive who I admired for his knowledge and wisdom. He was super smart and on occasion a charming guy. Unfortunately, there were also occasions when he let the stress of the job allow him to lead by fear and intimidation. We were in a full staff meeting with a room full of my peers and colleagues. I asked him a question, and he blew up at me like a spoiled kid in front of everyone. I was fuming, but I did not address him in the room. Just by looking at their faces, I could tell everyone in the room, including the executives, felt uncomfortable and empathized with me. No one had the courage to call him out. So, I sucked it up and let the meeting move on.

When the meeting was over, I followed him into his office and slammed the door. I told him that I could not and would *not tolerate his behavior and that he needed to treat me with respect. I could tell he was shocked that I had the audacity to call him out. I was very low on the hierarchy compared to him. He put his head down and sighed heavily. He then said, "I am so sorry. I never meant to disrespect you." He then went on and confided in me that he was under tremendous pressure at work and wasn't getting along with his leader.*

*I accepted his apology and advised him that his tirades made him ineffective as a leader. I pointed out that in my short time in his department, I noticed that his team simply tolerated him, but if given the choice they would never work for him. He asked his assistant to cancel his next meeting, and we talked for over an hour. In that moment, we gained a mutual respect. I not only received the apology I demanded, I gained an advocate and sponsor in his business. He subsequently went to bat for me to receive a promotion into management in another department. If I had not had the courage to speak up for myself, he would have had no guidelines on how to treat me, and I would have enabled him to treat me badly. Never be afraid to speak up and set standards for your life.*

*Warm regards,*

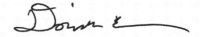

## CHAPTER 9

# An Unbearable Life

Y DAD'S FUNERAL WAS one of the biggest homegoings that I ever attended. There were so many people there, it was impossible to grieve. My mom and Mona got into an argument about who would sit in the family car. My mom and dad never divorced, so she was still officially his wife. My mom insisted and jumped in the car with me and dared anyone to tell her she could not. I was in a daze, but I remember the police escort to the cemetery and looking at the procession of cars following the family to the gravesite. The procession was, with no exaggeration, six blocks long. I remember thinking my dad was loved by many. I was in a daze and somewhat emotionless until we got to the graveyard.

After the prayer and everyone picking their flowers, we headed to the car. Suddenly, it hit me like a ton of bricks. This was it. I would never see my dad again. I tried to make it to the car, but my emotions got the best of me. My knees hit the ground, and I wept uncontrollably. I had experienced physical abuse, been kicked and beaten, but THIS... it was a pain that my heart could not endure. It was the most gut-wrenching pain I had ever felt. Maurice picked me up and helped me to the car. My mother tried her best to console me. It was truly a sad day for the entire Jones family. Their beloved Bubu was gone at the age of thirty-five.

Maurice and I started going through a series of challenges. He began seeing a woman a few years older than him. I was a loose cannon and looked for any opportunity to physically fight him. Once, I jumped out of his car as he drove down the street, rolling at least a block, scraping the skin off my legs. I even pulled a gun on him and chased him out of the house. I was unraveling quickly, and he did not and could not provide the emotional healing that I desperately needed. Soon after, we began to grow apart quickly. To make matters worse, someone pulled a stunt that would seal the deal. Someone broke into our home and stole all of Maurice's shoes. There had to be at least 100 pair in his closet. Someone stole all of them, our DVR, television, and even my underwear. They did not touch the money, guns, or drugs in the house.

Barron and I were the first to discover the robbery. When Maurice came home, he accused me of setting it up. I was appalled and thought, This idiot must be stupid. Why in the hell would I steal his shoes and not take the money, drugs, guns, and jewelry? Is he high? This fool must be crazy! What in the heck am I going to do with a bunch of men's shoes that I could not wear? We had a terrible argument and decided to break up. A few days later, I found a pair of my panties, with a picture of Maurice and me with a big red X on it, in my coat pocket. He agreed to pay my rent if I got an apartment, and at this point, I was done. He had begun using drugs, and obviously his judgment had been severely altered. His being with another woman hurt, but I honestly could empathize and understand. My mess was deep and complex, and he had his own mommy issues to deal with. We were not mentally prepared to deal with our issues as a couple. Our relationship had run its course. Our season was over.

Tammy and I had subsequently visited a tarot card reader for fun. The woman told me that someone was trying to put "roots" on me, but my soul was too strong. When Maurice and I broke up, he subsequently ran into a string of bad luck, which was exacerbated by his addiction to drugs. The tarot card reader also told me I would marry and have three children and a successful career. I thought it was rubbish back then. But, looking back, she had nailed it. What she envisioned surely came to pass.

At the age of seventeen, I was a broken and despondent little girl longing for peace. My father had died, and I was ridden with guilt over my last encounter with him. I would give anything to have told him I loved him before he died. I had broken up with someone I had once loved and cared for deeply, and my mother had disappeared without a trace after my father's funeral. So, there I was living in a small studio apartment in Irvington. Maurice would come to check on me and bring me money on a regular basis. I tried to keep myself busy hanging with Tammy and a few close friends. A few months went by and still I had not received a single phone call, visit, or note from my mother. I assumed she was dead and no one had found her body. There was no way in the world my mother would not check on me, especially knowing that I was still grieving my dad's death.

I wanted to die. My depression resulted in me rationalizing that my parents were in heaven, so if I killed myself we would all be together. I visited Beth and Pop's house and took a bottle of pills off Betty's dresser. I took a handful and swallowed them. An hour later I could not stop going to the bathroom and felt so dehydrated that I kept drinking water. It turned out that I had taken an overdose of Lasix water pills. All I got from my effort was a bad case of running to the bathroom.

Having been unsuccessful with my first attempt, I decided that I had to do it right. I went to the local drug dealer by my apartment and purchased a 10-on-10 of opiate pills (enough to kill an elephant). On my way home, I called Ethel to say goodbye. She lived over an hour away, so I knew she could not come in time to stop me. I took the pills and fell into a deep sleep. When I woke up, I was in the psych ward of East Orange General Hospital with a strange nurse staring me in the face.

After I had called Ethel, she had contacted Barron and told him to stop by my apartment to check on me. When he and his friend arrived, they had seen me unconscious on the floor through the window. They had kicked open the door, scooped me up, and Barron had tried unsuccessfully to wake me up. He told me he was never so scared in all his life. He had run to the car screaming at his friend to speed to the hospital. He told me he was hitting me as hard as he could, but I would not wake up. He had feared I was dead and began begging God to save me. I don't remember seeing him or getting my stomach pumped in the emergency room. All I know now is that I ended up in the psych ward.

As I assessed my surroundings, I began thinking, What the hell have I gotten myself into? There are crazy people all around me. I'm not crazy. I just want to go to heaven. I can't believe I'm stuck in this place. It's worse than the damn Projects. Everyone here is a nut job, junkie, or zombie. I'm scared. If anyone touches me, I'm going to snap. Over the next six weeks, I played along with the psychiatrist asking me stupid questions like, "Is the medication helping?" I wasn't taking the medication. If the doctor really knew anything about me or paid attention in my therapy sessions, he would have known that I was deathly afraid of becoming an addict, so I would never take drugs. I faked that I was taking the pills with the nurses and then threw them in the garbage. Sometimes I would even give them to the other patients. I remember thinking, I'm not fucking crazy; I need to get the hell up out of here. So, I stayed on my best behavior so I could be released before anyone figured out that I was not taking any of the medication. The therapy was helpful because it gave me a chance to share my feelings. But, I still wanted to die. ∎

## Dear Reader,

would like to share a wise quote by Michelle Ventor. "People come into your life for a reason, a season, or a lifetime. When you figure out which it is, you'll know exactly what to do."

I wholeheartedly believe that people come into our lives for a reason and a season. However, many of us struggle in knowing who is worthy of holding on to for a lifetime. We hold on to what could be and fantasize about the "what ifs" instead of letting go. We sometimes fail to take the time to learn from the lesson and move on with our lives. The enemy will send people into our lives to test our strength, character, and integrity. Make no mistake, we will all be tested. But our faith is the tool that God provides to see us through these tests. Those of us who walk strong in faith build the mental armor to handle difficult circumstances without succumbing to fear and without holding on to the baggage that prevents us from living a life of joy. It allows us to rejoice in the testimony of how we not only survived, but overcame to make it through. You see, survivors live in spite of still holding on to the baggage from the past. But, when you overcome, you succeed in spite of the obstacles and emotional turmoil, because you have left the baggage behind.

As I reflect on my experience with depression and attempted suicide, I must acknowledge that mental illness is a scary thing. Unfortunately, it is more common than we would like to believe. Many of us try to deny it exists within our families. People associate shame with mental illness and feel as though they will be vulnerable for letting the secret out to others. The fact of the matter is, at some point in our lives, we are all going to be faced with some serious life-changing events. If we are afraid to be open and honest for fear of judgment, we put ourselves at a disadvantage by failing to seek the support needed to cope with reality. We all need help at some point. Coping with the demons in our head that tell us we are not worthy or we should be ashamed can be exhausting.

Are you starting to see a pattern in my life? At the time I could not. I was too busy wallowing in my misery. Why is it that I was not dead or in jail? Because at every occasion when I should have succumbed to the challenges life threw my way, God intervened. But why? It would take me another twenty-five years to figure it out, and I will share the revelation with you later. But for now, I will share this, because I know it to be true. Surviving the most difficult times of your life is simply the test and preparation required to receive the blessing that is waiting for you on the other side. It's important not to wallow in the pain that you have endured. Embrace it as a badge of honor. It's a testament to the person you are destined to become!

Warm regards,

# CHAPTER 10

## *Facing My Demons*

WAS RELEASED INTO THE custody of Betty and Pop. The house had a whole different vibe. They were still visibly distraught by the death of their only son, my beloved father. Although she no longer suffered with alcoholism, Betty still had a mean streak. She was known to cuss out anyone who crossed her path. Pop tried his best to keep things together, but he was never the same after my father's death. Losing their only son was a heartbreak that could never be repaired.

My therapy in the psych ward did nothing to ease my pain. I was hellbent on killing myself. I sat in the living room thinking of my dad and imagining all sorts of things about how my mother died. Something strange would happen whenever I was in the room by myself. The television would turn off unexpectedly. I remember asking Ethel and Betty if it ever happened to them. They said no. I confided to Ethel that I thought my father was trying to let me know he was with me.

Ethel said, "You crazy. You done really lost your damn mind! I ain't gonna lie. Sometimes I feel Mama's spirit in the room. I guess we both are two crazy bitches." We laughed it off. We definitely felt a presence that could not be explained.

A few days out of the psych ward, I decided to finish what I had started, but it would never come to pass. I had decided to take Betty's blood pressure and heart medicine. I did my research and knew the mixture of pills would be sure to kill me. I snuck into Pop and Betty's bedroom and took two bottles of pills off Betty's dresser. I hid the pill bottles in the side of the couch cushion where I sat the entire day. Betty was cooking one of my favorite meals, pork chops and sauerkraut with red potatoes. My plan was to enjoy dinner and to swallow the pills after everyone went to bed. I watched rap videos on MTV while Ethel and Pumpkin helped Betty cook dinner. I listened to Boogie Down Productions's "My Philosophy" and Eric B. and Rakim's "Microphone Fiend." Once in a while, I would take a break to enjoy Betty and Ethel going back and forth with their normal banter.

Mary had moved to the suburbs of Lake Hopatcong, New Jersey, so she did not visit as often as Ethel. Pumpkin and I cleaned the kitchen before she left to stay with her boyfriend. Mimi was out with her boyfriend, and Ethel stayed a while to keep Beth and me company. Pop sat in his chair and drank a few beers, watching his favorite television shows before he and Betty turned in for the night.

The house was dark and quiet. As I reached between the seat cushion to grab the pills, a miraculous thing happened. Nana Jones walked from the doorway and stood right in front of me. She had on a white dress with flowers around her head. She looked younger and had a glow all around her. It was if I could reach out and touch her. She did not physically speak, but I heard her say, "God wants you to know that you are not responsible for your father's burdens here on earth. God has a plan and greater purpose for your life."

I did not know what to say. Before I could respond, she was gone. I remember thinking, *Am I freaking crazy? Did that just happen?* I knew she was an angel. She had come to get my father, and now God had sent her to stop me from taking these pills. I was confused. What was my purpose? What was I supposed to do? The only thing I knew for sure was that I could not swallow those pills. I tiptoed into Pop and Betty's bedroom and placed the pills back on the dresser. I suddenly had an overwhelming sense of calm, because I felt as if my life would turn out alright. I had no idea how, but I finally had hope for the future. What was I to do with the information Nana Jones had dropped on me? I needed more direction.

A few days later, I told Ethel and Mary about my vision. Ethel stated, "Heifer, you crazy!" Mary said, "Crazy as a fox." They both conceded that they too had experienced paranormal activity since Nana Jones's death. They advised me to keep it to myself. Ethel said, "Bitch, you'll land in the psych ward forever if you start telling people this shit." We all started laughing.

There I was, seventeen years old, and the only thing I was good at was sleeping with drug dealers and hustling. I wasn't opposed to working, but I was not going to work at some fast-food restaurant for chump change. I called Molly and asked her how old I had to be to get a job at the hospital where she worked. Molly advised that I had to be eighteen. I told her I needed to get a job badly. I just wanted to work. I asked Molly if she would help me get an interview if I brought in a copy of my birth certificate and it showed that I was eighteen. I believe she was so relieved that I had reached out to her that she would do anything to make it happen.

I arrived at the human resources department of the hospital where Molly worked as an executive assistant. In an attempt to mimic Molly's classic style of dress, I was dressed in a black suit and a pair of five-inch heels. Molly introduced me to the hiring manager, a black woman who appeared to be well-educated and was impeccably dressed. She called me into her office for the interview. She asked me a few questions, and the interview seemed to be going well. She then took her glasses off and looked me straight in the eye and said, "I love and adore your grandmother, and she loves you to the moon and back. I'm going to give you a chance. Please do not mess up. Molly is well respected here, and she does not need to be burdened with any unnecessary drama. Do we have an understanding?" I thanked her and told her she had nothing to worry about. I would never embarrass my grandmother.

I was hired as a unit clerk, making $10 per hour working the three to eleven p.m. shift. This shift was perfect for me. I was not used to waking up early, so it wouldn't be hard for me to keep these hours. The first person I met was a woman named Vanessa. She had a welcoming personality. She was tall and easy on the eye. Vanessa was assigned to train me for my job. She introduced me to the staff, including her sister Diane, who worked as a phlebotomist. Work was not bad. My colleagues were nice and there was no management around after six p.m., so we were free to joke around and goof off on occasion. Vanessa and I became fast friends. We would often go shopping and hang out at the club on the weekends. We were both into fashion and liked to dress nice.

Although I liked my job well enough, I still felt the need to hang in the projects with my old peers. Terrance was home from jail, and I would give him money to flip for me. He confided that he had feelings for me that equated to more than friendship. I already knew, but never thought about crossing that line with him. I valued his friendship and had no interest in jeopardizing my friendship with Tammy, even though they had both moved on.

When I was in high school, I was often accused of trying to take someone's man or envied by a select group of girls for having light skin and hazel eyes; as if my looks somehow made my life easier. I had so many fights over jealous girls' envy, it was freaking unreal. I even lost friendships over this nonsense. The fact of the matter is, I hated being attractive to men. Anyone who truly knew me would know that loyalty and trust meant everything to me, so I was not about to sleep with a friend's man just because I could. I had no love or trust of men. I had been disappointed and used too many times by a man to put their wants and needs before a true friend. I also had no qualms about what men saw when they looked at me. Sex was always on top of their minds. I won't go into all the details of my experiences with the opposite sex; that's a whole other book on its own. However, I will share a few encounters that affected my self-esteem and self-worth.

The first boy I trusted when I was new to the eighth grade, looking to fit in, told everyone that we had slept together. He was immature and treated me as if I were merely one of many trophies to sit on his mantel. I'm not putting all the blame on him. I was looking for attention in all the wrong places, seeking the relationship of a boy to validate my self-worth.

That same year, I was randomly attacked by some dude I did not know. My friends and I were hanging on Central Avenue. My girlfriend and I were walking back to her house to hang out and eat the chicken we had purchased from a local fast-food chain. This tall masked man came out of nowhere and hit me in the back of the head with an egg. My friend and I initially thought it was one of the guys we had just left on the avenue and that he was playing around. We quickly realized it was not. He was way too tall and did not laugh or speak a word. When we decided to run, he grabbed me and started banging my head against the brick wall. Then he proceeded to rip my shirt off. I could not scream because I was in shock. My girlfriend started throwing chicken at him. When he went to push her away, we both ran in opposite directions. She ran home to get her mother, and I ran to the house of a friend who happened to live close by.

I had to wear a brace around my neck for a few weeks. Pop was still a detective and went out of his way to find the perpetrator. He came home from work a few weeks later, irate. He asked me if I knew a boy named Dominique. I told him no, and he accused me of lying. I swore to Pop that I did not know this boy. Pop advised that he had pictures of me. He told the police that he was my boyfriend when they picked him up for questioning.

It turned out that Dominique was mentally ill and stalking me. He lived on the block behind our house and would take pictures of me through his window and follow me to school. Pop pressed charges, but because the boy was a minor and mentally ill, I was not allowed to attend the closed court hearing. I received a lousy $500 check from the Violent Victims Bureau.

To this day, I have no idea what he looks like and would have no clue if he stood right next to me. The only solace I have is knowing that Pop told Dominique's mother to move or he could not guarantee her son would not be found dead in an alleyway. Pop told me she got the message and moved down South. He said, "I would have blown his head off if he came near you again." Pop was a man of few words, but he meant what he said. He would have done anything to protect Mimi and me. He loved us to pieces.

In tenth grade, I dated a young man who I really liked. He lived in the apartment building right next to Molly. During this same time, a young man approached me randomly on the street and asked for my number. I told him I had a man and kept it moving. I would see him in the neighborhood every now and then, but thought nothing of it.

One night my boyfriend left me in his apartment and went out with his friends. I was frustrated because he took way too long to come back, so I left and proceeded to go home to Molly's house. It was late, but I wasn't concerned for my safety, I was going right next door. When I walked into the doorway, I reached in my pocketbook to get my keys. Suddenly, the door opened and on the other side of it was the young man who had asked for my number. He appeared to be intoxicated and grabbed my face and demanded I give him a kiss. I pushed him off me. He snatched the keys out of my hand. He told me he was not going to give me the keys until I gave him a kiss. I told him to keep the keys and proceeded to go back to my boyfriend's house. That fool punched me dead in my face. I went crazy. We began fighting, and he threw me against the wall, put his hands around my neck, and forced his lips on mine. Luckily, a couple walked into the building. He let me go and ran away.

Later that year, I was visiting friends and had begun seeing another man named Robert. He was very handsome and easy to talk to. He hung out with a few young men from around the neighborhood that I knew well. One day, his friend called me to advise that Robert was at his house and wanted to see me. I didn't think anything was strange. I knew they were friends, and Robert visited his house frequently.

When I arrived, Robert's friend told me that he was upstairs. I walked upstairs, and Robert was nowhere to be found. His so-called "friend" closed the door and told me he wanted me badly and had to have me. I tried to run past him, but he grabbed me and threw me down on the bed and proceeded to undress me. I fought him hard and could see he was becoming visibly angry. He put his hand over my mouth and became more violent. He ripped my bra open. He was going to rape me. I fought him as hard as I could. His bed broke and hit the floor with a loud bang, and he let me go. He called me a stupid bitch and told me to get the fuck out of his house. I passed his mother as I ran down the stairs and out the door.

The last and most disheartening story I will share is that of my encounter with my maternal grandfather. He was known to be fond of brown liquor and his love of the ladies. He was a handsome man with lots of charisma and charm. Nicky, my mom, and I visited my grandfather, who at the time was the superintendent of a luxury apartment building with a pool. I was fifteen at the time, and loved to swim. We spent a majority of the day at the pool. When we were done, I decided to take a nap while the grownups smoked weed and hung out in my grandfather's living room. My grandfather's girlfriend, who was younger than my mother at the time, was there with her young daughter.

I remember being in a deep sleep and suddenly being awoken by the brunt force of someone's hand grabbing my vagina. When I turned around it was my grandfather lying next to me, appearing as if he were asleep. I jumped up and ran. I immediately told my mother what had happened and that I wanted to leave. My mother confronted her father. She began screaming "What the fuck is wrong with you?" He responded, "I'm sorry! I was drunk and fell asleep. I must have been dreaming or something."

His girlfriend intervened and told my mother to calm down. They exchanged words, and my mother began to physically fight her. Nicky and I had to pull my mother off of her. The girlfriend ran in the bedroom and locked the door.

My mother began banging and kicking on the door. Nicky and I calmed my mother down, and we left the apartment. I remember my mother stating that her father had tried the same stunt with her, but she had chalked it up to his drinking. She told me he was drunk and he didn't mean it. Hmm, does being drunk give the trusted men in our lives an excuse to abuse us? I moved on, and we never discussed it again. I forgave my grandfather, but I never looked at him the same again. I dared not ever tell Molly. He had already broken her heart beyond repair.

It is estimated that one in four girls and one in six boys will be sexually abused before they turn eighteen. What would have happened if I did not immediately jump up and run out of the room? I understand the shame that comes with this type of experience. But the real shame is sweeping it under the rug and making excuses to downplay the behavior. It gives the abuser free rein to continue the abuse.

My self-esteem was shot as a result of these and many more instances I have not shared. I began to think something was wrong with me. I hated being attractive to men. I wanted to be ugly. These feelings were the start of my addiction to food and my spiral into obesity. I had no self-love or acceptance of who I was as a young woman.

Many people judge those who struggle with their weight, without any regard for their mental well-being. The worst thing you can say to a person who is struggling with obesity is that they need to lose weight. As if they don't look in the mirror every day knowing that they are obese. Your judgment about their weight does nothing to address the problem; it only makes it worse.

If you want to help, try being a friend who uplifts and inspires them to be their best. My husband is that friend to me. He's never commented on my weight, even when I ballooned to 300 pounds. He was there as I battled to lose over 100 pounds and never disrespected or criticized me. He's always told me, "I married you for your heart, not your physical appearance." Needless to say, he's a keeper. I no longer suffer from low self-esteem, but I will admit that managing my weight is still one of my biggest challenges.

When I became a married woman with children of my own, I mustered the courage to ask Betty why she made Pop put his paycheck on the dresser and issued him an allowance. I said, "You never worked. What made you think you should take all the money and leave him with a few dollars in his pocket?" She replied, "I could not stop him from cheating on me, but I'd be damned if I let him take money out of the mouths of me and my children to give to another bitch." In that moment, I could relate to my grandmother as a woman. We never spoke of Pop's infidelity again. They experienced fifty-three years of marriage before Pop passed away. I suspect they both made their share of mistakes, but in the end, their love for one another was undeniable. ■

# Dear Reader,

here will be times in life when you feel the pain is too unbearable to overcome. The death of a loved one is as bad as it gets. The fact is, we are all going to die. It's alright to grieve, but we cannot succumb to the grief to the point where we are not able to move on and live the life God has provided for us. It is a disservice to those we loved and a distraction from the life we are meant to live. I now choose to take the best parts of the loved ones I've lost. I honor their memory by using my life to serve and support others.

Betty sharing her vulnerability about Pop's infidelity helped us to bond as women. Ironically, I vehemently despised Pop's infidelity and its effects on Betty, but it did not diminish the love and respect I had for him as a man and my loving grand-father. Humans are flawed . . . point blank and period. Who was I to judge or insinuate my feelings into my grandparents' marriage. How Betty and Pop chose to resolve their issues in their marriage was between the two of them. Honestly, it was none of my business, and not my problem to bear. Are you holding judgment or grudges on events or incidents that are truly none of your business?

Warm regards,

# CHAPTER 11

# God's Ultimatum and the Battle to Control

WO WEEKS BEFORE MY eighteenth birthday, I was hanging in the projects with Terrance and some of our friends. We were on our way to Club Sensations in Newark. I had on my fur coat, a cute leather suit, door-knocker earrings, and wore my hair in what we referred to as the "Salt-N-Pepa" cut. As we walked down the street, detectives rolled up and threw us up against a brick wall to be frisked for drugs and weapons. While being frisked by the freak detective, who took advantage of feeling me up and licking my face, I heard a voice say, *You're going to be eighteen in two weeks. If you don't change something, you'll end up dead or in jail. What's it going to be?*

I believe this was God's ultimatum. He was telling me that I had to leave the street life behind. He would not protect me if I refused to be obedient. I went to the club that night and partied like it was 1999. I knew instinctively that this part of my journey was over. I had to leave the streets behind. Many people tell me that they never hear God. I question whether they are ready to listen. I am no theologian by any means, but I cannot fathom that if God spoke to me, he does not speak to everyone.

I once heard a quote from Pope Francis in which he said, "Obeying God is listening to God, having an open heart to follow the path that God points out to us." I have always been an observant listener. I refer to this as one of my gifts. I have come to learn that not everyone is able to block out all the noise in their heads and really listen. This gift has also helped in my journey to becoming a leader in corporate America.

The next day, I called Aunt Mary and asked if I could live with her in Lake Hopatcong. She was overjoyed. She picked me up that afternoon, and I never looked back. Mary was anxious to give me the love and support that I needed to thrive. Trey and I were glad to be reunited and living under the same roof. We were always ride or die for one another and the best of friends growing up. Trey, Mimi, and I had a special bond. When we were little, Aunt Mary would make Trey wear rollers in his hair and send us out to play. Mimi and I had so many fights with the neighborhood boys in our defense of Trey. The boys would pick on him and call him derogatory names. Trey was a pretty boy, with light skin and curly hair and the cutest baby face one can imagine. He was such an easy target for the roughneck boys in the neighborhood.

Trey was dating a phenomenal young woman named Tina from East Orange. Aunt Mary wasn't thrilled about her at first, but Tina grew on Mary. She came from a solid middle-class family, and she kept Trey in check and out of the streets. She and her sisters would visit often. Mary had a pool, so her house was the place to be in the summer. We would also walk to the lake on occasion to swim.

Vanessa and I grew close. I would often spend weekends at her house and got to know her family well. Vanessa's brother Thomas was smitten with me. He was a widow, seven years my senior. He had married his teenage sweetheart and lost her to lupus two years before. I never disclosed to Vanessa that I hustled drugs on the side when we first met. Vanessa was a single mother and would never take part in illegal activity. She came from a close-knit family. She was one of five siblings. Her mom was a strong woman who did not put up with any nonsense. She immediately took to me and treated me as if I were one of her own children. She would often tell me that I would be perfect for Thomas. At the time, I paid her advice no mind. I was not feeling Thomas at all. Looking back, I can honestly say, a mother knows best. Thomas and I have been together for twenty-eight years, and married for twenty-four as I write this. He's my soulmate. He has loved me through my deepest and darkest days. Albeit, I did not make it easy. He chased me for a year before I finally gave in. I'll elaborate on that later.

Aunt Mary was not thrilled with my friendship with Vanessa. In fact, she had made up her mind that Vanessa was on welfare with two kids, and began telling the family that lie. Mary had become so controlling, she literally began to lose her mind. She began to dictate what Trey and I could wear, what we could eat, and what friends we could have. She needed to control every aspect of our lives. I did not realize it then, but looking back, I believe she was suffering from mental illness.

Mary spent her entire life trying to keep the family intact. At this point in her life, she had lost her parents and three siblings. Her oldest son rebelled and became addicted to drugs. His first wife was a lovely woman, but she was not Mary's choice for her son. The family would often tell the story of how Mary showed up at their wedding wearing all white to spite the bride. Mary was a character indeed. She set the example of how the more you try to control something, it ultimately controls you.

I put in the work to take myself out of the street life for good. But now I had a new problem. Although Aunt Mary loved me, she became so controlling, she tried to force me to live her dream. My dreams were irrelevant to her—not because she wanted me to fail; it was the opposite. She wanted me to win so bad, she thought she had to control every aspect of my journey. Mary had become my dream killer.

So, there I was living in Lake Hopatcong, still working at the hospital and trying to manage Mary and her need to control every aspect of my life. Mary was also a lot of fun, so it was not all doom and gloom. We had great times and enjoyed spending time with one another immensely. I also came to the realization that I might not ever see my mother again, which deeply saddened me.

Six months after my eighteenth birthday, Molly called me at work with horrific news. My mother had been arrested for prostitution. She was picked up on Frelinghuysen Avenue in Newark. I felt ambivalent. I was relieved to know that my mother was alive, but I was also disgusted that she was selling herself to men in exchange for drugs. We bailed her out of jail. After she was released, we hugged one another and cried. I could tell my mother was deeply embarrassed and ashamed. She had never wanted to hurt Molly and me in this way. She excused herself to the bathroom and disappeared without a word or a goodbye.

I became enraged. I called Aunt Mary to advise that I was spending the night at Betty and Pop's house. I stole Pop's service revolver and called a friend to ride me around to find my mother. I neglected to tell her that I planned to shoot my mother in the head. I decided that I would rather see my mother dead than selling her body. I searched for hours, walking into crack houses and known drug areas. My mother was nowhere to be found. Looking back, I

cannot believe how arrogant I was. The nerve of me thinking I had the right to kill my mother. At the end of the day,
she was still a child of God. Who was I to have the audacity to judge my mother's journey and decide her fate?  ∎

## Dear Readers,

Although Aunt Mary loved me dearly, I've come to realize that sometimes the people in your life are not capable of seeing or accepting the vision you have for yourself. I am a firm believer that you must surround yourself with like-minded people who support you and your dreams. Family is sometimes your biggest deterrent because they lack your vision. Never let anyone distract or deter you from pursuing your dreams. Your path and purpose are distinctly different and unique. If God put the vision in your head, you must put in the work to make it happen. Sometimes that requires loving your family from a distance. Not everyone is meant to walk beside you in the journey.

We read and hear in the news way too often about people who cannot reconcile their anger and heartbreak. These feelings can consume you to the point of no return. I certainly don't condone the murder of anyone. But I understand how the complexity of those feelings, combined with an inability to cope, can lead to horrific outcomes. My mother certainly did not deserve to die by the hand of her daughter. I am so grateful that the woman I am today would never contemplate taking a life. I celebrate people and life. Time is too precious to waste sitting in judgment and a false sense of superiority. The fact of the matter is, we are all flawed individuals trying to figure out our purpose in this life. We can't control people, but we can control our attitude and how we choose to love and celebrate one another.

Warm regards,

# CHAPTER 12

## *Grown and Fed Up*

HEN VANESSA INTRODUCED ME to Thomas, I was not impressed. He was a nice guy, with a beautiful smile and the smoothest chocolate skin, but I was not feeling him romantically. We would see each other on occasion, and I was always polite. One day, Vanessa invited me to a family barbecue. We were having a great time, and out of the blue Thomas asked me to go for a walk. I obliged, and as we were walking he began to tell me all the things that were special about me. I kept thinking to myself, This fool is running so much game right now, no way am I buying it. When I told him I wanted to go back to the barbecue, he said, "Okay, but I need to tell you something first." I was curious, so I listened as he said the infamous three words: "I love you."

Now remember, I had no trust in men and I just knew he was running some serious game. I replied, "What? You don't even know me. How are you going to fix your mouth to say you love me? Boy, bye!" I began walking fast back toward the crowd, but Thomas wouldn't leave my side. He smiled and said, "That's okay if you don't believe me. But you'll see. Just wait." I remember thinking, *This nut must think I'm stupid.*

Well, Thomas made it his business over that year to show me that he meant it. When Vanessa and I went to the

club, he would miraculously show up. If some guy asked
me to dance or got too close, Thomas would approach
them. "Yo, my man, that's my girl. Keep it moving." I would
get so mad at him. He did not care. He gave me my space,
but he clearly marked his territory. This went on for months.
He literally wore me down. The day after Thanksgiving,
we were at a party. Vanessa and I were on a double date
with these guys we had met a few weeks earlier. When I
walked in the door with my date, Thomas walked up to
him, and yet again said, "Yo, my man, that's my girl. You
need to leave." That punk took one look at Thomas and
told me goodbye.

That was it. I was tired of playing this game with Thomas,
so I decided to give him a chance. Well I concede, it was
the best decision I ever made. My dad once told me that I
should never chase a man. He said, "The man that's right
for you will chase you." He was right. I put Thomas to the
test, and he continued to chase me. He often tells me, "I
fell in love with you at first sight. I always knew there was
something special about you."

It had been three months since we had bailed my mother
out of jail. She finally got the nerve to go out of her way to
find me. Aunt Mary told me that she called and asked if
she could come by and speak with me. Mary was thrilled.
She always had a soft spot for my mom. I had mixed feelings but was willing to see her.

When the doorbell rang, Mary was excited. I guess she
envisioned a heartfelt, miraculous reunion. Well, when she
opened the door, there was my mother hideously dressed,
with blue eyeshadow and red lipstick overtaking her small
face. There were also two white women by her side dressed
in a similar fashion, all of them strung-out and a little fright-
ened by what they were about to walk into. Mary was
gracious and welcomed them into her home. She called

me to come downstairs. Trey came barreling up the stairs from the basement to be nosy. He met me on the stairway and asked, "Yo, what the fuck?" I shrugged my shoulders because at that point, it was what it was.

Aunt Mary and I did not know what to say. The two women with my mother went on and on about how my mother loved me and always spoke highly of me. Mary offered the ladies something to eat and escorted them into the kitchen so my mom and I could have some privacy. My mother told me she was addicted to crack. She also explained to me that she could not function on crack. She said the drug was so addictive, she spent her entire day chasing it and would literally do anything to have it. She told me she had to disappear because she had hit rock bottom and did not want me to see her in that state of mind.

She swore that after seeing me and Molly, she had made up her mind to go to rehab. She said, "After seeing you and Mommy, I know I have to kick this addiction to be back in your lives. I need you." She wept, and I had little emotion. Quite frankly, I was disgusted by it all. She could tell my heart was cold. She begged me to forgive her. I sat there unbothered by the drama. Mary quickly interceded and said, "Rin, look at your mother. I'm so proud of her. She's getting herself together." Mary gave me a look that said, *You better be nice.* I rolled my eyes and said, "I wish you all the best. I hope the rehab works."

At this point in my life, I was in a loving relationship with Thomas. I was ready to move on with my life, with or without my mom. I was tired of the ups and downs, and I was now unwilling to deal with the consequences of my mother's addiction. It was a burden that I did not deserve to carry. No matter how much I loved my mother, I had no control over her ability to cope and beat her addiction. It was something she had to do for herself, on her own. I gave her a hug and wished her well. Aunt Mary gave my mom and her friends a goodie bag of food to take with them.

Thomas worked as a kitchen manager in a popular restaurant. He worked long hours, but we tried to spend as much time together as we could. My relationship with Thomas did not sit well with Mary. She despised him at first. She assumed he was a drug dealer and forbade me to date him. She was delusional, telling the entire family that he was a drug dealer. He was a hardworking man with no desire to go to jail. He wanted to settle down and have a family. I was astonished by her blatant lies, but everyone in the family knew Mary was crazy. Whenever Mary went on one of her tirades, Ethel would say, "You know that bitch is crazy as hell."

When I told Mary that I was moving out to be closer to Thomas, we got into a huge argument. Mary finally lost her damn mind for real this time. She pulled out a knife, pointed it at me, and said, "I'll kill you before I let you ruin your life." I yelled to Uncle Chuck, "You better get this crazy bitch." I ran to the basement and pulled the shotgun out of the hall closet and pulled the action on the gun, so she knew I was serious. I told her, "You better put that knife down, or I'll shoot your crazy ass." Uncle Buck had showed us how to hunt when we were kids, so handling that shotgun was not difficult for me.

Mary was crazy, but she was not stupid. She knew I would pull the trigger before I would let her stab me. She gave the knife to Uncle Chuck, and I put the gun down. She sat on the steps and cried hysterically. The real issue was not Thomas at all. She did not want me to go. She had become accustomed to having me around and would miss me terribly. Uncle Chuck called Beth and Pop and asked them to come and get me.

Betty called Vanessa and asked her to drive her and Pop to pick me up. Betty did not drive, and Pop did not like to do so at night. Thomas tagged along to keep them company on the forty-five-minute commute. When Betty arrived, she looked at me, smiled, and said, "You should have shot the crazy bitch." Thomas and Vanessa were visibly astonished by the whole experience.

Pop told Thomas, "You want to be with a Jones woman, this is a day in the life. All of them heifers are crazy as hell, and you better sleep with one eye open." Thomas was not discouraged at all. Vanessa, on the other hand, could not contain her feelings. She blurted, "Y'all crazy!" Eventually, Aunt Mary and the entire family came to embrace and love Thomas. He is a great husband and father and has the biggest heart of anyone I know.

I moved back home with Pop and Betty and eventually, Thomas and I moved in together. We were excited about the future and anxious to start a family. Thomas had confided in me that he was not the best husband to his first wife. He promised God that if he had a second chance he would be the best husband he could be. Like all couples, we had our ups and downs. But at the end of the day, our love and bond were unbreakable.

My mother did it! She kicked her addiction to crack and was back working as a legal secretary. She had an apartment in the complex where her dad was superintendent on Prospect Street in East Orange. Pop helped Thomas and I obtain an apartment in the same complex. I became pregnant with our first child and excited about the future. Thomas worked nights and did not want me to work while I was pregnant, so I quit my job at the hospital. Thomas was a good provider, so I did not want for anything. I was happy and content.

I remember our first night in the new apartment. I spent the day unpacking. I took a nap and woke up around midnight to cook Thomas dinner. I expected him home around two a.m. after the restaurant closed. When I turned on the kitchen light, I nearly died from a heart attack. There was not one, not two, not four, but literally a dozen mice on top of my kitchen counter. I began screaming and ran out of the house. I banged on my grandfather's door. He opened it and said, "What's wrong with you?" I told him we had an infestation of mice. He replied, "Oh, you didn't know?" He began laughing hysterically. I did not find it funny. I was tempted to slap him. I called Thomas and told him we had to move. I advised him that I was staying with Pop and Betty until we found another apartment. Thomas did his best to calm me down, but I was not having any of it.

The next day, Thomas brought home a cat, so I no longer had to worry about the mice. We named the cat "Buttons." Her first day in the house, she killed a mouse and put it in front of our feet as if it were a gift. We never saw another mouse again. We had found a solution, but I was still adamant about moving to a different apartment.

We found a nice place in Orange, and I was excited about becoming a mom. Thomas accompanied me to every doctor's visit. My doctor always had a long line of patients, so we knew it would be a minimum of an hour's wait each visit. Thomas would go to the store and bring snacks for the ladies in the waiting room. There was a select group of pregnant women who looked forward to Thomas and me visiting the doctor.

A few days after we moved in, I lost the keys and Thomas and I were unable to locate the superintendent to let us into our apartment. We decided to spend the night at Betty and Pop's house. When we arrived at the front door, it was off the hinges. Anyone could have walked right in. Barron had been staying with them for a few weeks. He had split from his wife and needed a place to stay in the area. Ethel and his dad lived thirty minutes away.

Barron had gotten into a shootout with undercover policemen in Newark. The Sheriff's Office had issued a warrant and the taskforce had broken down the door and entered the house with guns blazing. Pop, Betty, Ethel, Barron, and one of my cousins happened to be in the house at the time. They had all watched in horror as policemen threw Barron down to the ground and hand-cuffed him. The police then tore up the house searching for the gun.

While a few sheriff's officers were searching the home, the others told my family members to stand up to be frisked. Everyone complied except Betty. Ethel laughed as she told Thomas and me, "This crazy bitch almost got us all locked up. The cops told her to stand up to be frisked. She told the police to kiss her ass and refused. Luckily, they found the gun and backed off of Betty."

Barron was later indicted and found guilty on fifteen counts, which included conspiracy to commit robbery, aggravated assault, hindering apprehension, attempted murder, and unlawful possession of an assault weapon. He was sentenced to an extended term of life imprison-ment with twenty-five years parole. Barron's sentence was a blow to the entire family, but especially to Ethel. Knowing she would never see her son outside of a prison was devastating.

Our rational brains understood and did not excuse the fact that Barron had to face the consequences of his actions. However, this did not outweigh the fact that our hearts were broken. The fun-loving Barron with the colossal spirit, infectious smile, and big heart was gone. I am sharing Barron's story because this could have been me. Anyone who believes they can commit crimes and not face the consequences is delusional. I guarantee you crime can and will ultimately lead you to two outcomes: prison or death.

I went to visit Barron when my second child was two and my oldest was eight. My oldest, Janae, had to be searched because she wore a jacket. She told me she felt very uncomfortable. In that moment I decided to never take my children to prison. I did not want them to think that visiting someone in prison was normal or acceptable. I did not want my sons to believe that leading a life that would result in prison was acceptable to me and my husband.

I am in no way judging Barron's journey. In fact, I believe his upbringing prevented him from having the choice of leading a life without crime. His father and role model was one of the biggest gangsters on the East Coast. Although Ethel did not commit crimes, she condoned them by allowing her husband to expose her children to the life. Fast money, nice material goods at your disposal at any time, being renowned as an icon by your peers—why would anyone second-guess choosing that life?

During this time, my mother began borrowing money from us on a regular basis. She'd normally be broke the day after she got paid. Although she was never a good saver, something was off. She always paid us back, but I began to suspect that she had relapsed and was back on crack. She would make excuses that her car had broken down or that she had had to pay her rent. She was lying, but the truth would soon come to light. ■

# Dear Reader,

e live in a society that tells us we are entitled to instant gratification. Many of us lack the social maturity to delay our gratification based on what is best for our lives long-term. When you combine a lack of patience, moral value, faith, and no options, it will ultimately lead to an outcome similar to Barron's. I am a strong believer in paying it forward. I know if Barron had the opportunity, he would do whatever he could to prevent young men and women from following in his path.

I understand that part of my purpose in life is to share my story with at-risk youth to demonstrate that success is possible. When children are drowning in hopelessness, despair, and lack the proper role models in their lives, they cannot envision how to create a path to achieve a life of joy and success. This is why I am passionate about bringing awareness and advocacy to at-risk youth and their parents. We as a society must work to provide more alternatives through mentorship, community education, behavioral health, empowerment, and job placement programs.

Are you doing all you can to fulfill your life's purpose? How are you giving back? Are you holding on to a dream or vision in your head and hesitating to make it come true? What's stopping you? Life is short. Don't be distracted by complacency and fear. It is easy to live a good life and let "the good" rob you of being GREAT! It takes courage to step out on faith and to make the vision or dream in your head a reality. Just ask *yourself, Was I born to be good and mediocre, or great and extraordinary? You are the only person who can determine if you are living up to your true potential.*

*Warm regards,*

# CHAPTER 13

## Tough Love

At eight months pregnant, I was so anxious to give birth to my first child. Thomas advised that we should start planning our wedding after the baby's birth. It wasn't what I envisioned as his proposal, but I was thrilled that he wanted to marry me. I had no desire to be a single mother, and I had forewarned him that I would not play house forever.

One evening the phone rang, and it was my mother. She told me she was in a bind and needed my help. I asked her what she needed. "I got put out of my apartment, and I need to stay with you and Thomas until I can get on my feet," she said. There it was. She was busted in her lie. A month prior, she told me she needed to borrow money to pay her rent. Obviously, she was not paying her rent. I called her on it. I asked her if she was smoking crack again. She denied it, but she knew there was nothing dumb or stupid about me. She was caught red-handed.

I had too much at stake. I knew what would happen if I let my mother stay with us. She would begin stealing and lying. There was no telling who she would let in our house when Thomas and I were not home. I was not having any of it. I did not hesitate to tell her, "HELL NO!"

I said, "Mom, I love you, but I love this baby in my belly even more. I cannot let myself or this child suffer through the consequences of your addiction. I can't do it. If you don't clean yourself up and get off that crack, you will never see me or my child again. I promise you, I'm not playing!" I abruptly hung up the phone.

Thomas could not believe that I would not let my mother come and stay with us. He said, "Dee, how are you going to put your mother out in the street?" I knew he could never understand. I replied, "You have to trust me. Saying no to her was hard for me. But you've never lived with a drug addict. I can't have my baby around her. I don't want my child to think her behavior is acceptable or normal. I'm praying that she's sick and tired of living with this demon. She has to muster the courage to clean her act up. We can't help her; she has to help herself."

Molly turned her down as well. A few weeks later, my mother called to inform me that she was staying at the Salvation Army Homeless Shelter and she had entered a rehab program. She asked if I would come to one of her therapy sessions. I agreed. I was a week overdue in my pregnancy and scheduled to have my labor induced in two days. I was nervous and excited at the same time. I arrived at the therapy session, anxious to get it over with. My mom looked good. Her doctor told me she was determined to get her life together. The thought of losing me really scared her.

My mom told me that her biggest regret was failing me as a mother. She wanted to make up for lost time. I knew she was sincere. At that end of the day, I could never deny her love for me. She told me that my saying "no" was the best gift I had ever given her. It was her love for me that gave her the strength to beat her addiction to crack. This time, my mother kicked her crack addiction for good.

I delivered my daughter on October 18. I did not think I would make it through labor. The nurses did not give me anything for the pain. It felt like a Mack Truck continuously driving through my stomach and out of my behind.

It was the most painful four hours of my life. Thomas tried to hold my hand, but due to the pain, I had the strength of ten men. He said, "Dee, you can't squeeze my hand. You're going to break it, and I won't be able to work." I did not argue. He was right.

He sat by my side, scared to death. He asked the nurse to give me something for the pain. She said, "The monitor doesn't show that she's in labor." I screamed back, "Fuck the damn monitor. I'm about to die!" When she checked me, it was too late to give me any medication. I was already dilated eight centimeters. She immediately called my doctor. He was headed to the hospital from the roller-skating rink, his favorite hobby.

A few minutes later, I felt the baby's head between my legs. I told Thomas to hurry up and get the nurse. She took one look and had me rushed to the delivery room. My doctor walked in the room just in time to catch the baby. There was no pushing. This child was hellbent on saying hello to the world. It was a sweet girl! We named her Janae. She weighed seven pounds and had a head full of curly, thick black hair. Thomas and I were so thrilled to meet our baby girl. The entire family came to visit and meet Janae. Molly and my mom were the first to arrive.

Molly was surprised. She said, "You're sitting up in the bed. You just had the baby a few hours ago." I felt fine. I had had a natural birth, no stitches, and as soon as they put Janae in my arms, the pain I had just endured was a distant memory. When we arrived home, we saw that Molly had stocked our apartment with a wall full of diapers and a ton of clothes. She was overjoyed to be a great-grandmother. I enjoyed being a mom. I always wanted children. I hated being an only child and often dreamed of having a big family.

My mother visited every week and showered Janae with gifts. She was still working at the law office and living in a rooming house in East Orange. She began dating a man she met at lunch. He was a contractor, Cuban, a really nice guy who pampered my mother with money and gifts. He was also drug free. The only issue I had with this relation-ship was that he was also very married.

When Janae was six months old, I told Thomas that I had to get out of the house. I was tired of watching *Barney* all day. I needed to be around grownups. He encouraged me to go to school to get my GED before going back to work. I took his advice. He was now working the day shift, so I went to school at night to ensure he was home to watch Janae. The old 1979 blue Buick I drove finally died. Vanessa gave us her car and purchased a new one. Vanessa and I also decided to go into business together and began sell-ing lingerie to bring in extra cash.

We hit the male strip club on the weekends and booked parties. We did well. Those women in the club were a wild bunch. They began to look forward to Vanessa and me coming in with new lingerie each weekend. We also coor-dinated fashion shows and charged people a small fee to attend. Both Vanessa and I were good at entertaining. We knew how to create great parties.

I passed the GED test with flying colors. I had always been good at taking tests. I obtained a job at Elizabeth General Hospital and did well. I started as a unit clerk and applied for a higher position transcribing oncology orders. Although I was really good at it, working on the oncology floor was hard for me. I became too attached to the patients; and when they died, it took too much of an emotional toll on me.

The oncologist I worked for encouraged me to post for a new, higher-paying position that had opened in the operating room, so I did. I got the job as operating room scheduling coordinator. It was exciting at first. I basically ran the operating room—I ordered supplies and controlled the schedule. The surgeons were extra nice to me. They all wanted prioritization on the schedule. I learned a lot working in the OR, especially to mark my own extremities if ever operated on. There were multiple occasions where the nurses did not know right from left, which led to several lawsuits.

I eventually left the hospital to manage a doctor's office, and from there I landed a role in home health care and climbed the ladder quickly. I held the title of director of Patient and Employee Services. I spent the majority of my time getting the company prepared for accreditation. That meant I had to create all the policies and procedures for the employees and patients. I also coordinated the first ever Home Health Care Symposium for the state of New Jersey. The job was demanding, but I loved working in a high-paced environment. I even hired Thomas's youngest sister, Melody, to work as the office manager. The owner of the agency was a charismatic man who built his business from the ground up. I admired his hustle and desire to become wealthy and leave a legacy for his family.

The time came when Molly was celebrating the finalization of her divorce. Years earlier, when she and my grandfather were still together, he treated her horribly. Molly came home from work after thirty-six years of marriage and six children to find her belongings packed in a U-Haul. Some woman greeted her at the door and advised Molly that she had moved in. Molly was forced to sleep on the sofa of her oldest son until she could save enough money to get an apartment. My grandfather had cleaned out her bank account and had run up all of her credit cards. She was forced to file for bankruptcy. I admired Molly and her ability to rebound and work through the turmoil. Molly is a class act!

I remember asking her, "What did you do when the woman opened the door to your house and told you she had moved in?" She replied, "I told her she could have the sorry bastard, and I left." I knew this was rational behavior, but the Jones in me was baffled by her reaction. Had this been one of the Jones women, that house would have been burned down with my grandfather and his girlfriend in it. Molly taught me the real meaning of strength. It took more strength for her to walk away than to fight.

She said, "Honey, you have to learn how to pick your battles. Not everything is worth fighting for. I certainly felt angry enough to fight that woman, but I didn't deserve to be in the gutter with the pigs, so I walked away." My mother mumbled in the background, "If I was there, that bitch would have got fucked up." I turned and grinned. Molly simply shook her head and said, "What am I going to do with you, Weesee? Don't use that language in my house!"

Thomas and I married in September 1993. Janae was seventeen months old and loved to dance. She literally closed the dance floor down at our wedding. The day started out rainy. We rented a hall, and Thomas's friends from the restaurant volunteered to cater. There were 200 friends and family in attendance. Many of them I did not know—Betty had invited everyone and their mama. Molly picked up a large majority of the expenses for the wedding. She recovered from the bankruptcy and did well saving and getting back on her feet.

My mother sang a beautiful rendition of "Inseparable" by Natalie Cole. On our way to the park to take pictures, the limousine carrying my grandfather Bernard and my mom had disappeared. My grandfather had insisted on stopping by the liquor store to buy a few bottles of Scotch. I was so mad but quickly got over it after Thomas began joking about it. When we returned to the reception, everyone was having a splendid time. We danced the night away. Two of my distant cousins, a mother/daughter duo who I met for the first time at my wedding, got terribly drunk and fell on the dance floor. I was mortified. Betty and Ethel thought it was funny. Ethel told me, "Stop being so damn uptight. Tell those men over there to go help those two drunk bitches up off the floor."

Thomas and I honeymooned in Atlantic City. His siblings came along the first evening and crashed in our room. When I woke up that morning, one of his sisters was asleep in the closet and the others were spread out on the floor. We didn't mind. We enjoyed their company. We all laugh about it to this day. Thomas won $3,000 on the slot machine the last day of our honeymoon. Soon after Thomas and I were married, Molly, my mother, and I decided to pool our resources. Molly purchased a three-family house. She occupied the first floor, my family occupied the second, and my mother lived on the third. We lived under the same roof for the next sixteen years.

My son TJ was born in June 1997. My labor with him was much different than what I had experienced with Janae. It was tolerable, but he was not as anxious as Janae to see the world. The doctor had to literally pry him out. When they put him in the incubator, we heard a loud noise. TJ had grabbed the side of the incubator with his hand and had begun shaking it. I remember the doctor saying, "What the heck! Is this baby BAMM-BAMM?" My husband was overjoyed. He had a son, and all was good with the world. TJ was the cutest baby ever, with big dimples and curly hair. I had to watch him like a hawk. Everywhere we went, strangers would ask to hold him. I was not having it. Janae was happy to be a big sister and immediately bonded with her brother.

Although I had only gained twenty-five pounds during my pregnancy, I quickly put on an additional

thirty pounds months after TJ's birth. I ballooned to 240
pounds. At this point, I avoided looking at myself in the
mirror. What was the problem? I was not unhappy. I had
a great marriage, my career was thriving, and I was in
control of every aspect of my life . . . except my weight.
Before I knew it, I was pregnant with Timmy. He was born
in September 1999. His birth was the one and only time I
received an epidural during labor; I experienced an aller-
gic reaction that caused me to shake uncontrollably. I
was terrified that the shaking would never stop. It was
an awful feeling. Thomas was right by my side, reassur-
ing me that everything would be okay. Timmy was the
smallest of my three children. He weighed six pounds,
five ounces and had skinny legs that kicked nonstop. He
looked like a mouse, but immediately won my heart. Now
that he's a teenager, he reminds me so much of my dad.
There have been a few occasions where I have caught
myself looking twice, because for a split-second I saw
my dad in him. People who knew my dad often say, "He
looks just like Bubu," when they meet Timmy.

It makes me smile, believing that my dad is smiling
in heaven at his beautiful grandchildren. I would give
anything for my children to have known him. Cherish the
fond moments with your family, because they are few
and far between. Tomorrow is not promised to anyone.
Spend more time enjoying the love, laughter, and fond
memories. Through the dysfunction, I have come to see
that those cherished moments with family are a gift that
will last forever in your heart. I have fond memories with
Molly's children, who came over for brunch every Sunday.
We have lots of fond memories of living in that three-family home, including waking up to the smell of my mother
smoking weed every morning before work and in the
evening before bed.

My mother and I were very open with my kids about her struggle with addiction. We wanted my children to understand that they were genetically predisposed to inherit the disease of addiction. We had many discussions on the importance of saying no to drug use. A few months after Timothy was born, I began to suffer from postpartum depression. It was a really weird experience. I felt like I was outside of myself looking in. I did not have any harmful feelings toward Timmy. I hated myself and the person I had become. There was one instance where Thomas came home from work and I had disappeared. He was frantic looking for me. He eventually found me in the closet crying and praying for God to help me.

We went to my doctor and told him my symptoms. He advised that if my symptoms did not subside in a few weeks, he would prescribe medication. Thank goodness my symptoms went away a few weeks later. This may have been prompted by the doctor advising that I would need medication. I did not want to be dependent on a drug to help me regain my sanity. I also decided to get my weight under control. I went to a nutritionist to discuss my options and decided to have lap band surgery. Over the next year, I lost one hundred and thirty pounds.

I also learned about another aspect of my family history during this time. Thomas and I entertained the family on most holidays. We had a catering business and knew how to cook for large groups. My grandfather Bernard and his sister were in my living room cutting up. They both loved the brown liquor. They started reminiscing about their childhood and how they had chauffeur-driven limousine rides to school.

I said, "Wait, what? How could that be? That was the 1930s." My grandfather said rather flippantly, "Oh, we were rich." I was shocked. I said, "What do you mean you were rich?" They then went on to tell me and my children how their father had emigrated from St. Kitts at the age of sixteen and had become a wealthy businessman in Newark. They told us they lived in a mansion on Bergen Street where University Hospital now sits. Their father had a music school, attended by the legendary jazz great Sarah Vaughan. He owned multiple supper clubs, taverns, and property. He was also a board member of the Newark YMCA.

Their father died under mysterious circumstances in 1940, and his wife was not business savvy. She remarried. Her new husband was an alcoholic, and they squandered the money. They also advised that their father was rumored to have saved the life of a famous white mobster and was provided money and protection for his good deed. This was not hard to believe. Dutch Shultz and other famous mobsters were known to frequent the jazz clubs and restaurants in Newark during that time. My uncle told me that when they were young, Bernard would often get money from a gangster nicknamed "The Boot," who was fond of my great-grandfather. Bernard tried to follow in his father's footsteps, but his love of women and booze outweighed his desire to become a successful businessman.

I began to think, *How is it that my great-grandfather was a wealthy man in the 1930s and yet by the time my mother was born in 1953, there was little to no evidence of his legacy?* Was it a coincidence that I happened to work for one of the largest financial services companies in the globe, based in the same hometown as my family? I think not. I believe part of my purpose is to honor my great-grandfather's legacy. I chose to do this by dedicating my work to educating and providing access and resources to underserved communities. I became determined to change this narrative for women and communities of color. I am proud to say that I use my gifts and talents to help women and communities of color learn how to create a plan for intergenerational wealth.

During this time, we also received another blessing, albeit I did not see it that way at first. Janae had been what people would call the ideal daughter until she hit high school. In her freshman year, her grades began to slip and she was staying out past curfew. Thomas and I became worried. We decided to enroll her in a private Catholic high school sophomore year. She was not happy. Two weeks in, she came home and said, "You think this school is better? All these kids get high all day. All I did was party at the town high school. My friends and I were not getting high."

She knew how I felt about drugs, so she knew she would get a reaction. I said, "Those kids can get high, but if you do, I'll break your freaking neck! Are we clear?" She rolled her eyes, sucked her teeth, and walked away. She eventually got acclimated at the new school and did well. She enrolled in college, and Thomas and I thought we had overcome any serious issues with Janae. Well lo and behold, we would later find out that she had dropped out of college and was seeing a young man that she knew we would not approve of. On top of that, she hid her pregnancy for six months. By the time we found out, she was well into her pregnancy. Like it or not, Thomas and I were about to become grandparents. Thomas literally had a heart attack and ended up in the ICU for five days.

My response: *I want a freaking refund for all the high school tuition we paid to prevent this from happening.* We eventually came around and embraced the fact that we were going to become grandparents. The birth of our granddaughter turned out to be one of the biggest blessings in our lives. Janae named her Nevaeh—heaven spelled backwards. We nicknamed her "Shugz." She's now the pride and joy of our lives. ■

*Dear Reader,*

*olly's experience taught me that walking away from the dysfunctional people we love is never easy, but always worth it. If you keep yourself in a dysfunctional environment, you become part of the problem. Not everyone will appreciate what you bring to the table. If you are constantly giving and all you receive is hurt, it's time to walk away. If the people in your circle don't add value to your life, subtract them.*

*Janae taught me and my husband a valuable lesson about parenting. You cannot plan your children's lives. You can guide them, set boundaries, and expectations based on your unconditional and never-ending love. But at the end of the day, they are going to become adults and make decisions for themselves. The unexpected birth of my granddaughter turned out to be one of the biggest blessings God bestowed on our family. My daughter hid her pregnancy for months because she feared disappointing my husband and me. She knew we had a different plan for her life. The truth is, God had the ultimate plan and we had no say. It was never our intent for our daughter to be fearful of confiding her truth to us for fear of our judgment. We are grateful that she now understands that our love for her could never be diminished. Judging a person does not define who they are; it defines who you are.*

*Warm regards,*

# CHAPTER 14

## *Faith over Fear*

FTER I HAD MY second child, I decided to leave the home health care company. The job was way too demanding and put a strain on my family life. I signed on with a temporary agency and was assigned a position at a large and well-respected financial services company. I worked in the systems area as a project manager. I did well and was eventually hired full time as a medical underwriter. I moved up the ladder quickly. I worked in several departments and volunteered to work on diversity and inclusion initiatives that provided me exposure to senior executives, some of who eventually became my advocates and sponsors.

My mother was still addicted to heroin. She needed it to function more than to get high. She worked and for the most part had a normal life. She was falsely diagnosed with fibromyalgia in 2005. The doctors treated her badly. They thought she complained of the pain because she wanted to get high on pain medication. Nearly a year later, she called me at the stairway screaming. I ran upstairs and there was blood everywhere. She passed out in my arms. I screamed for Thomas to call an ambulance. When she arrived at the hospital, she had to have a blood transfusion. After they ran a few tests, she was finally properly diagnosed with stomach cancer.

The entire family rallied to help my mom beat the disease. The oncologist advised that they wanted to conduct surgery to remove the melanoma. I refused. I told them I wanted my mother to be discharged so we could get a second opinion. I took her to Memorial Sloan Kettering **Cancer Center.** As I suspected, the oncologist at Sloan disagreed with the original course of treatment. She recommended oral chemotherapy and radiation. The oncologist explained the course of treatment and what to expect. She also advised that she needed to run a few tests, which included HIV.

When the doctor left the treatment room, my mother began to cry. I asked her why. She said, "I never told you this, but the reason I started using crack after your dad died was because everyone we shared needles with had died from AIDS. I know I have HIV. There's no way I don't."

When the tests came back it was revealed that my mother did not have HIV. In that moment, she realized that she had fundamentally tortured herself and had become a crack addict and a prostitute for something that never existed. I remember thinking how foolish my mother was for never taking the damn test. Her lack of faith and courage had completely derailed both of our lives. And for what? False Evidence Appearing Real. That fear demon is real, and if we don't face it, we can be fooled into a false belief. In that moment, I vowed never to lose my faith or succumb to fear. This ultimately became one of many gifts that my mother gave me.

My mother completed her cancer treatment and went into complete remission. Both of my sons played football, basketball, and baseball, so my mom would often join us on the weekends for one of their many games. She was their biggest cheerleader. She did well at work and was promoted a few times. No matter how much money she made, she never saved it. My mother drove me crazy by being irresponsible. We both purchased Kia cars in 2001. I paid cash for mine; she put money down and had a car payment of $300 that she could barely afford. She spent a minimum $100 a day on heroin to keep herself going. She neglected to pay her car insurance and totaled the car.

So, what did she do next? She purchased a new Lincoln with a ragtop and a $750 per month car note. I remember when she brought the car home. I asked her how she could afford it. She said, "Don't worry. The payment isn't much more than my old car."

I knew better, but what could I say. She was going to do what she wanted. She went to work every day and deserved nice things. I eventually found out the real cost of her car note after she was arrested for driving with no insurance. I had to bail her out of jail. When I took her to the insurance agent to get car insurance, she had to reveal the amount of the car note. I never said a word. I just shook my head in disbelief.

Every birthday and Christmas holiday, she showered my children with lavish gifts. But most importantly, she gave them the biggest hugs and kisses and told them she loved them every day. She treated my husband as if he were her son and loved him dearly. Although my mom was flawed, she had the biggest heart of anyone I knew. We took a family vacation in August 2010. We embarked on a seven-day cruise to the Caribbean. There were sixteen of us, including Molly and my mother. Our first stop was Barbados. When the cruise ship docked, we rented a tour bus to explore the island.

My mother jumped in the front seat, right next to the driver. I knew she was up to something. Sure enough, she had asked the driver to score her some weed. I pulled her to the side. I did not want Molly to know what was going on.

I said, "Ma, my kids and Molly are on this bus. What if the police come? I'm telling you now, if you get caught, I don't have any bail money for you. You are on your own. I am going to keep it moving and enjoy my vacation."

She frowned. I could tell she thought I was a party pooper. I was a nervous wreck thinking what would happen if she got caught. She somehow made it back on the ship without the weed being detected. On the fifth day of the trip, she ran out of spending money. She ordered a glass of wine at the family dinner. She then yelled at Thomas and me across the table, "Son, Rin, I ran out of money. This is on you!" We shook our heads and laughed.

My cousin, my mom's nephew, turned to Molly and asked, "Where did she come from? She's off the chain!" Molly giggled and replied, "I don't know. She's always been outspoken."

As we matured, our mother/daughter dynamic was interesting to say the least. I was the responsible one, always thinking ahead. My mom was the carefree spirit who lived in the moment. She couldn't care less what people thought about her. The evening before we arrived home, I told my mother to flush the remaining weed down the toilet. She responded, "Hell no. This is some good weed!" I advised her that when we got off the boat, customs agents would be in the luggage area with dogs. They would certainly smell the weed. I warned her that if she got arrested, I would not bail her out. I then said sternly, "Flush the weed before you leave this ship!" She reluctantly agreed.

Sure enough, when we exited the ship, the customs agents were there with the dogs. My mom smiled at me and said, "I'm glad you made me flush the rest of that weed." Little did we know that would be our last family vacation together. ∎

*Dear Reader,*

y mother's experience in life taught us both to face
our fears and to be courageous in the pursuit of
our dreams. I used this insight to enhance my life,
advance my career, and climb the corporate ladder.

When I started my career in corporate America, I was completely content working in my cubicle cranking out the work. I
kept my head down and stayed to myself. I am extremely observant, and I read people well. I quickly came to realize that I
could do the work of the managers just as well or even better.
There were many who walked around with fancy degrees and
big titles and with no common sense or interpersonal skills;
and some really were lacking when it came to working and
leading with integrity. I knew I could lead teams just as well
or better than many of the individuals I observed. I was not
arrogant. I was confident.

When I had the vision to pursue a leadership role in corporate America, I knew I could never be complacent with being
average and mediocre. I can't tell you how many times I have
heard other colleagues tell me, "I want a career change," "I
want to get promoted," and "I do not understand why my
career is stuck." They are so busy talking and complaining
about what they want, they begin to waste their time and
energy becoming part of the problem. They are not willing
to put in the work required to achieve their dreams. In most
cases, it is simply because they are unwilling to overcome their
fear of failure and the unknown.

I have never been qualified on paper for the positions I
applied for and became successful in. I applied because I knew
I was capable and what I did not know, I could learn quickly.
The worst that would happen is that I could fail, and I was
willing to take the chance and learn. Always remember that

when you become complacent with what you have achieved, you have placed self-imposed limitations on what God says you are truly capable of.

I stepped out on faith and began volunteering for projects that would demonstrate my ability to lead. As I mentioned, I knew the worst that would happen is that I could fail. I built relationships with the key players and decision makers. They became my advocates and sponsors, opening up doors and opportunities for me to climb the corporate ladder. You see, the street and corporate codes are similar. You look out for someone in the street, they look out for you. When you make executives look good to their peers and upper management, they will want you in their circle and will advocate for you.

Warm regards,

## CHAPTER 15

# *The Gift of Forgiveness*

N AUGUST 2011, THOMAS and I purchased a new home in South Orange. Our move was bittersweet. We did not want to leave Molly and my mom, but we needed more space. My mother's oldest sister moved into our apartment, which made our transition much smoother.

In late September 2011, my mother began complaining of shortness of breath. She told me she could barely walk up the stairs. The emergency room doctor falsely diagnosed her with pneumonia. Her symptoms became worse. She would come to my house often to watch movies on the big-screen television. She was an avid movie buff. One day as we sat on the couch, she lifted her shirt and said, "Do you feel the bumps on my back?"

I did not have to feel them. Immediately, I saw that she had knots the size of golf balls. I said, "Mom, have you been to the doctor?" She said, "Yes. I have lumps in my breast as well." I called and got her an appointment at Sloan Kettering right away. I assumed her stomach cancer had come back and spread.

It had not, but this time she had a carcinoma and was diagnosed with Stage 4 cancer. The doctors were not sure where the cancer had originated, but it had spread rapidly. She started chemotherapy immediately. A few weeks later, the doctors would discover the cancer had originated in her lungs. The family took turns driving her to Sloan for her treatments. I was fortunate that my company allowed its employees to work remotely. I would try to schedule my time so that I could work out of the office as I sat by my mom's side during chemotherapy.

My mother relied on my judgment and immediately gave me power of attorney to make decisions on her behalf. She was determined to beat the cancer. She did not want to die. She completed her final round of chemotherapy in late January 2013. We were optimistic that the doctor would give us good news. I prayed every night that God would stop my mother's suffering. She would cry for hours about how bad her bones hurt after the chemo treatments. The morphine the doctors prescribed did not help. Also, she was still taking heroin. She no longer smoked weed. She told me the weed made her feel nauseous.

When the doctor called us into her office, I could tell she had bad news. With tears in her eyes, the doctor said, "The cancer has spread to your brain. This cancer is aggressive, and the chemotherapy is not working." The doctor recommended that we consider hospice care.

My mother responded, "Can't we continue with the chemotherapy?" The doctor looked at me. My mother was not ready to hear what the doctor was telling us. "Mom," I said, "the chemo is causing you so much pain. I think you should come stay with me and Thomas. You cannot continue to walk up and down those stairs." She reluctantly agreed.

I now had the awful task of telling Molly and the rest of the family that my mother was dying. Mom was Molly's baby. This would be the second child that Molly would lose to cancer. Mom's older brother had died from the disease two years before. I brought my mother home and got her settled into bed. I went downstairs to Molly's house and asked my aunt to come down. I told them that my mother's prognosis was poor and that I was going to move her into my home as soon as the hospice care delivered her bed and supplies.

They wept and hugged one another. I called Thomas to let him know what was going on. He and my sons removed the couch from our media room to make room for my mom's bed. We had a full bathroom on the first floor, so my mom did not have to walk up the stairs. Her bedroom, the kitchen, and bathroom were all on the first level. A home health aide came every morning to assist my mom with whatever she needed.

Molly and her siblings visited every day. At night, my mother and I had some deep conversations about life. She told me that she was not ready to die. She cried and told me that she felt so bad because she did not deserve my love. She felt that she had so much to make up for. She apologized for not being strong enough to leave James. She told me that she was so proud of the woman I had become. She said, "I know I have nothing to do with it."

I was stunned. Although we had our struggles, my mother definitely made many positive contributions to my life. She taught me to speak up for myself, to be kind, and to help others. In that moment, I knew I could give her a gift that I was unable to give to my father in his last days—the gift of forgiveness.

I told my mother that there was nothing to regret or to make up for. I understood that what had happened to me throughout my childhood was the preparation I needed to become the woman I am today. I said, "I hope you know that I do not blame you for any of it. I love you so much, and I forgave you a long time ago." The tears ran from her eyes; she did not have the strength to sit up and hug me. So, I reached over the bed and hugged her tight.

I asked her what she wanted for her funeral. She said, "Music. I want people to celebrate my life." She also wanted a closed casket. She told me she wanted people to remember her in her prime. The cancer had taken its toll on her body, and she did not like the way she looked.

She confided that she often would fake being asleep when Molly and her siblings visited. She said, "I cannot bear to see Mommy's face. I see the sadness in her eyes when she looks at me. I wish I was a better daughter to her." I told her that I knew for sure that Molly had no regrets. Mom responded, "I can't say goodbye."

I asked my mother if she believed in heaven. She said, "I don't know. I believe my spirit will live on." I told her that I looked forward to her being reunited with my dad. She smiled and said, "Me too." She added, "Make sure my grandchildren remember me." I responded, "You already did that." My children adored my mother.

The evening of April 20, 2013, my mother took her last breath and went home to glory. I called Molly and my mother's siblings so they could view her body before the funeral home picked her up. I immediately went into planning mode. The day after her death, I went through her purse and found twenty packages of heroin. I flushed them down the toilet and smiled. Her battle with this demon was over. She no longer had to suffer the mental and physical anguish of her addiction. I believe my mother's addiction to heroin and subsequent off and on use of methadone, prescribed by doctors to help her maintain her addiction, had contributed to the cancer that had invaded her body.

My mother's funeral was beautiful. Her coworkers, friends, and family had so many nice things to say about her spirit and kindness. My cousin played "Reasons" by Earth, Wind & Fire on the saxophone. A woman from the local church sang a medley of gospel songs. My children tried their best to be strong. My sons were two of the six pallbearers who carried my mother to glory. When we got into the limousine, my oldest son, TJ, began to cry, which set off my other children, who also began to cry. TJ is a stout and very macho-looking dude, with a thick beard and mustache. To see him cry was sad.

The reality of my mom's death had not hit me yet. I was so busy consoling everyone else and making sure her homegoing was flawless. It hit me like a ton of bricks a few months later while I was at work. I was having a challenging day, so I did what I would normally do: call my mother to vent. Midway through dialing her phone number, I remembered she was gone. I closed my office door and had the biggest meltdown. Luckily, it was the end of the day, and I did not have any more meetings scheduled. I waited until seven p.m. to leave the office. I did not want anyone asking me what was wrong.

The next day, I received a text from one of my mother's dearest friends since high school. It read, "Weesee and I spent a lot of time running the streets. Yet, all I remember is her kindness. In the early '90s we were stopped on Park Avenue by the police. I was working at the post office and would lose my job if I were arrested for drug possession. Weesee told the police everything was hers and saved my job. She was working for a private lawyer and even got them to represent me. All charges were dropped! Even in her last days, she would call me and ask if I was okay. I went away to upstate New York, and the last communication I had with her, she called me for help. She was dope sick and had no money. I sent her $150. She sent me a card thanking me and it was not long after that you called to inform me of her passing. We were never intimate, we never argued, we were just two knucklehead dope fiends who often talked about how lucky we were to have such wonderful daughters. We shared some private and real things with each other. Weesee was actually the best friend I ever had."

That message was so timely. It was the reminder I needed. I was no longer sad, although my mother's death was a devastating loss. I took solace in the fact that she had died with the peace of knowing she was dearly loved by her daughter. My ability to forgive, my faith in God, and knowing that I had the fortitude to put in the hard work when needed, were the biggest blessings I could give my mother.

I recently reconnected with Nicky. I'm so happy to report that she's been clean and sober for twenty-three years as of this writing. She has a successful career in law and is a homeowner and a faith warrior. Nicky told me she attributes her blessings to God and my mom and is now advocating to help addicts. We both wept as we shared memories of my mother. She told me my mother was special because she was a rare breed of an addict. "Weesee never lost her humanity. She was always a step above the rest of us because her family loved her unconditionally. Molly and her siblings loved her through it all, and it made a difference. They never judged her, and because of that, she was always a cut above. She was different. All of us in the street looked up to her."

Nicky also told me that she believes my mother was connected to God in a special way. "Weesee never had the hardness of the heart that addiction gave to the rest of us. She was always kind and generous. For the majority of addicts, the drugs ultimately rob us of our humanity. It is the only way we can cope with the awful things we will do to get high."

Nicky told me about her experience with James. She said, "I had the good sense to be afraid of James. He literally chased me out of your apartment. He wanted to control Weesee. He didn't want her to love anybody but him. He was so jealous. He hated you and Molly. He was a dangerous man and an alcoholic." That information took me by surprise. I never remember him drinking, but I was young, so I don't remember all of the details. They all met because of their addiction to drugs, but James's mixture of drugs, alcohol, and low self-worth must have been the right formula for his demonic behavior. I have learned to forgive him, but I will never forget the terror he inflicted on me and my mom.

I asked Nicky if she knew of my mom's experience with prostitution. To my surprise, she said, "Yes, she was involved with a pimp named Prince. He had about six girls, and he put your mom on methadone to control her addiction. He would not let her have contact with you. It was his way of controlling her. All she talked about was you and her love for you. He knew this was her weakness. At the time, I was so strung out, I didn't feel anything. Weesee tried to help me become functional by being part of his circle. He realized I was too strung out, so he kicked me out, because he could not control me. As soon as I got the money from a john, I would spend it to get high. Weesee's love was bigger than the disease. The fact that Molly and her siblings loved her through it unconditionally mattered. Your aunts and uncles intervened many times to help your mother."

Nicky also advised that my dad did such a long time in jail, but when he came home, they often hung out together. "At the time, I was married to my ex-husband, who was no good for me. Your dad was the first to recognize that I was in over my head. He said, 'Get out of this game now before it takes everything from you. You are not cut out for this life.' " I knew that my mom and dad remained friends, but I did not know the extent. They were ride or die until the end, which explains a lot about the decisions my mom made.

Nicky then proceeded to tell me about the brilliance of my mother. She said, "Your mother was serious about her music. The gentleman producing her and the band she was with were behind the times and didn't know how to maximize her talent. Your mother was on the brink of greatness. She was working with one of the musicians from Sly and the Family Stone. They cut records and demos. She was so dedicated, driven, and ambitious. Her looks, beauty, and talent were undeniable. She was kind, funny, and full of wit and full of humility. There was no mean bone in her body. Her only weakness was that she was a magnet for pretty-ass controlling men, like flies to honey. Weesee convinced me to pursue a career as a legal secretary because they made more money. She was smart. She told me, 'Being an average secretary is not good enough.' She taught me how to train myself and build a niche in law. She's the reason why I have a successful career today.

"In our prime, we were fabulous, make no mistake," Nicky continued. "We dressed to the nines. Your mom's beauty and presence, combined with my arrogance, meant we never had to stand in line to get in the club. The combination of Weesee's star power and my arrogance made us fierce. She had that quality where everyone wanted to be around her. I remember being on the dance floor with these fly-ass white boys partying hard and suddenly their model girlfriends came through to grab them up because they were jealous. There was one occasion when we went to see Parliament and the Funkadelic. We were in the limo with Billy "Bass" Nelson and got bombarded by the paparazzi. We were scared to death. In our minds, we were just hanging in the car with someone from the group. We had no idea they were so big that we would be hounded by the media. We had to literally run and duck into a small opening of the garage door to get back stage to the concert.

"We once attended the Budweiser Festival and were backstage with Aretha Franklin and Luther Vandross, who was not that well-known at the time, but had just written 'Jump to It' for the diva. We were backstage with Luther, Ashford and Simpson, Roberta Flack, and the stars in their dressings rooms. Luther was so humble and so nice. They all loved being in the presence of your mom. James put a wedge between me and your mom because of his hatred. I felt abandoned. It got better once he was gone. I remember your mom being so oblivious to the fact that one of the male cast members of *Dream Girls*, Obba Babatundé, was totally smitten by her during that time."

Nicky told me, "You are smart like your mom and super savvy because of her. Your story needs to be told. People need to know that we can recover—the addict and the family. The story does not have to end at a funeral. Addicts must dig up the old baggage and face it. We must learn to forgive our past mistakes to become free. In my darkest times, I heard your mother say, 'Get up. Don't give into the fear and depression.' "

Nicky encouraged me to tell my story so that other addicts can muster the courage to beat their addiction so they do no put their children through the experience that I had to endure.

I wrote this book to honor my parents. I wanted to control the narrative and help people understand the complexity of the dysfunction associated with drug addiction. My parents were good people who made bad choices. We live in a society that punishes people for their addiction, opposed to offering help and alternatives. I could have taken the easy route and chosen to follow in my parents' footsteps. However, there was always an inner voice and higher power leading me in a different direction.

Recently, a good friend asked me if I thought everyone was chosen. I had to think about that for a minute. The answer is no. Not everyone is chosen to do God's work. I was clearly protected for a purpose. I remember being on the road with Pastor Soaries a year ago. I said to him, "I have no idea why God has provided me with so many blessings." He looked at me like I was silly and said, "That's easy. God blesses us so we can bless others. You are constantly giving back, so he blesses you. It's not rocket science, my dear."

In that instant, it was clear. Part of my purpose is to share my journey so that it will help others. I believe that integrity and self-worth are fundamental character traits that can help anyone take positive actions, while vulnerability has the opposite effect. I turned my vulnerability over to God and found the strength and courage required to break free. I have come to understand that in those crucial moments in life, you must have courage and faith. The strength you need is inside of you and no one else.

I'll share a quick fact with you: I found out my name means "Beautiful Gift." I believe part of my purpose was to provide a gift to my parents—to share their story, to honor their legacy and sacrifice. Some people who read this book may not think my parents' lives had much meaning. But I know sharing this story will help many. The drug epidemic in the United States is reaching record-breaking numbers. People, regardless of race or socioeconomic status, are struggling with how to deal with family members addicted to drugs.

I was fortunate that I never used drugs. There are so many people who grew up in similar circumstances who chose to continue the cycle. I place no judgment on them, as I understand how they can feel like their circumstances were too insurmountable to overcome. Addiction is a chronic and relapsing brain disease that can be healed. As a society, we cannot and must not judge. We must come together and help those in need regardless of race, gender, or socioeconomic background. I believe that there is more power in unity than division. This is not a black or white issue. It's a human rights issue that burdens us all. We must unite to find a solution.

I was never satisfied with simply beating the odds. If you or someone you know is going through a tough experience, I hope these affirmations I share help you find some peace. These steps can help anyone address any obstacle, no matter how destructive you perceive them to be. I pray sharing my story helps to bring a successful outcome to your life.

**Forgiveness** – It is a process, not an event. It is your ability to let go of the shame, anger, resentment, or whatever feelings you have that are heavy on your heart. The more you hold on to those feelings, the more they weigh you down. In the end, it is you who suffers. It won't always be easy. But the more you go through the process of forgiving, you'll soon find that the things that may have burdened you in the past roll off your shoulders more easily.

Once I truly forgave my parents and all the circumstances that led to my depression and anger, I was free to live a life of joy and abundance. A male colleague at work once said to me, "I hope you don't get offended, but you are like one of the dudes; you don't hold grudges. We can disagree, and the next day, it's business as usual. There's no cold shoulder or attitude."

Now, I could have pointed out that his comment was sexist. But I understood where he was coming from. The truth is, when you have gone through hell and back, you tend to put the small, minute things into perspective. The issues I face at work are nothing compared to the life I have lived.

**Fortitude** – You have to put in the necessary work and take yourself away from the people who are bringing you down and be willing to make sacrifices to do it. Stay away from dream killers, and surround yourself with people who do good things for you and others.

When my mother asked to move in with me after losing her apartment due to her crack addiction, I had to make the tough choice of saying no. I had to be willing to sacrifice the loss of my mother in my life for my own peace and sanity. I could no longer enable her behavior and be witness to her destruction day after day. Sometimes you have to love people from a distance for your own sanity. I had to be courageous to help her understand she had to make a choice. Her love for me is how she fought the crack addiction. This doesn't mean that you stop loving people. It means that you put your peace of mind first. If you are not at peace, you are no good to anyone, including yourself.

**Faith** – Understand that your life has a purpose. My faith helped me understand that God wanted me to be more than a woman who lacked integrity and moral character. My life was meant to accomplish something big.

Remember that having faith is not about religion. It is about your confidence and ability to trust in a higher power. It's knowing that you can walk into challenging circumstances and come out stronger and better. It is trusting that you can walk through the door of opportunity even though you don't know what is on the other side. My faith helped me understand that the only limits in life were those that I placed on myself. I became fearless in doing what I needed to do to make things happen. There were so many times in my life when I shouldn't have made it, when I was told that I couldn't make it. But God said I could, and he protected me. ■

## Dear Reader,

Throughout our lives, we are often groomed to pursue the dreams and ideals of those who raised and influenced us. We are told to follow the path that they prescribe for us. The truth is we are all born with our own unique gifts and talents. You can attempt to walk the same path as someone else. I guarantee you, you will not end up in the same place. We each have our own personal journey to walk.

Therefore, you must take the time to understand who you are, what you have to offer, and create a plan that will enable you to live your own distinct and unique life of purpose. God's blessings for you are yours, and his blessings for others are theirs. Be humble and grateful for the good things in your life, and do your best to return the favor . . . God's favor!

With Peace and Love,

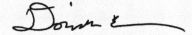

# Seven Life Lessons

INSPIRED BY WEESEE

THERE ARE SO MANY things that can be said about my mother's life. When I decided to take this journey and write about my life, I had no idea how therapeutic it would be in helping me understand the complex relationship I shared with my mother. This process has been very spiritual. It has allowed me to reflect on what I have learned about womanhood, humanity, forgiveness, and faith. Here are seven lessons I've learned from my mother's life journey.

## LESSON ONE

Let go of the SHAME! It's a simple word, yet powerful emotion that convinces us that we are inadequate and unworthy. The disease of addiction was the one burden my mother could never overcome. She carried the shame of her addiction for the majority of her life and acknowledged it was her biggest regret in life.

I once carried the heavy weight of shame by doing whatever I could to cover up my deep feelings of unworthiness. My biggest embarrassment entering corporate America was that I had not finished high school nor obtained a college degree. I was ashamed to admit this to my colleagues and peers. I forgot the fact that despite my shortcomings, I was a smart, intelligent, and capable woman who climbed the ladder to earn the title of vice president.

As a black woman in corporate America, I was quite often the only person of color in the room. When you are the "only one," and you do not have the same educational credentials as your peers, it is easy to succumb to feelings of inadequacy. During small talk and friendly conversations with my peers, I found myself praying that the subject of college or my childhood would not come up. My colleagues would often speak proudly of their college alma mater and their solid family upbringing. I dare not admit that I was raised in chaos and dysfunction, that I once sold drugs to earn a living, and spent time in the psych ward. I was determined to be evaluated based on my contributions, not my family and educational background.

Although I was very proud of my career accomplishments, I was still holding on to the baggage and shame of my past that continued to weigh heavy on my heart and in the pit of my stomach. Despite that, I had accomplished things that many people aspired to do but could never achieve in their lifetime. I did not need validation from other people to prove that I was worthy of my accomplishments. You see, I had already been qualified by God.

I just needed to sit down and reflect on all the blessings in my life to fully embrace the woman I am today. I am Weesee's daughter! I am a talented and smart wife, mother, and spiritual warrior with a successful career that serves many underserved communities. My mother carried enough shame for the both of us, so there is no need for me to hold on to useless baggage.

Here's what I know about shame: It is our fear of being judged and not liked or accepted by others. It is being afraid of showing our flaws and vulnerabilities. The truth is that everyone has a past, a story, or a painful event that has shaped their lives, whether it be addiction, abuse, financial woes, or some failure that they find hard to let go. To get past these feelings of unworthiness, we must establish the emotional maturity to be unapologetic in admitting that we are beautifully flawed.

## LESSON TWO

Have standards for who and what you accept in your life! When my mother realized she had become addicted to crack, she made a conscious decision to remove herself from my life. I did not realize it then, but she made this sacrifice to ensure that she did not derail my life.

I believe the experiences we shared up to that point taught her a valuable lesson. She was no longer willing to allow me to suffer the consequences of her bad decisions. Not everyone in your life will have the foresight to walk away when they cannot add value to you. How many times have we witnessed people struggle to get rid of the negativity in their lives? They endure bad behavior from family and the people they perceive as friends out of a misguided sense of loyalty.

If you claim to be an adult and consistently allow yourself to be in the presence of people who deplete your joy, you are an enabler with no standards or boundaries. You have the power to control who and what you accept. This includes family. The most courageous thing you can do for yourself is learn how to love people from a distance. Not everyone is meant to go on your journey with you.

Be prepared. People will call you selfish, stuck-up, or uncaring to make you feel ashamed or guilty for prioritizing your own needs. You cannot succumb to guilt for doing what is necessary for your mental well-being and success. If you're not at peace with who you are, you will be no good to anyone else. It is okay to love yourself, to be confident in who you are, and to be unapologetic for having standards for who and what you accept.

## LESSON THREE

Don't be complacent with being good and mediocre. Complacency is the destroyer of your ability to pursue your dreams! My mother always encouraged me to strive for more. Whenever I hit a roadblock, she would say, "You are too smart to settle for good, to give up or give in. Figure out how to make it work." What she was really instilling in me was to never settle for being good when I could be great! One of her biggest regrets was settling for James. She could have been a singing superstar, but she enabled James to distract her from pursuing her dream.

I am a firm believer that when God puts a vision in your head, there's nothing else to do but work to make it happen. I can't tell you how many times I have heard people say, "I want to write a book," or "I want to start a business," or "I want to change my career," or "One day I'm going to do it." They talk about their dreams but never take the first step to put in the work required to achieve them. In most cases, they are unwilling to overcome their fear of failure and the unknown.

When God sent Lily to tell me he had a different purpose for my life, I had no excuses and neither do you. Remember this quote that I often refer to when I feel like giving up or just settling when I know I can do more: "The killer of great is good." Don't settle for being good when you were destined to be great! The choice is yours.

## LESSON FOUR

Always be your authentic self! We were all born with our own distinct and unique gifts. The path that worked for me may not be the one that works for you. Life is guaranteed to throw obstacles your way. But remember, where there is no struggle, there is no strength. We should not wear our struggles as a badge of shame on our hearts and allow them to hold us back.

In my mother's final years, she had become unapologetic in who she was and was not afraid to speak her truth. It's something I truly admired about her, and she inspired me to stand tall in my womanhood. My mother's life was so much more than her addiction. I am honored to be her daughter.

I hope that you take the time to reflect, to celebrate what you have learned from your experiences and your ability to cope, and move on. Reflection will help you understand who you are and what gifts you have to offer the world.

The infamous quote "There's no testimony without the test" holds true. To truly heal, you must be willing to give the testimony and accept your past without fear of judgment. Those experiences made you the person you are today. Hold your head up high, speak your truth, and embrace the person you are and the gifts you offer to the world!

## LESSON FIVE

Accept that people are flawed and imperfect! I can honestly say I never witnessed my mother sit in judgment of anyone. She loved people and accepted them for who they were, flaws and all. I admired that about her. She really understood human nature. She never gossiped about others or put herself in a place of superiority. If she had a problem with you, she would tell you to your face and not mince words. I suppose the life she led gave her good perspective on people. I asked my children what lessons they learned from Nana Weesee. They responded, "Treat people with respect, and don't let anyone take advantage of you." My mother was a petite four-foot-eleven fireball. She would give anyone her last dollar, but piss her off and you would think you were in a brawl with a ten-foot giant. She was definitely a spitfire.

My mother would always tell me to be honest with people and tell them how you feel. You can't make assumptions about what people think and feel if you are not honest with them. This is probably why I have no patience for people who fail to be transparent. Tell it like it is, and accept the outcome. This doesn't give you permission to be rude or disrespectful. It simply means communicate with integrity and respect. This was one of the most valuable life skills I learned from Weesee. It's an integral part of the woman I am today.

## LESSON SIX

Be sure to give back and treat people with respect. With all of the deep pain, sadness, and embarrassing moments in my mother's life, she still found the strength to love and give back. My mother consistently demonstrated that she had a big heart. I witnessed her give her last dollar to a stranger on the street in need.

I remember being in a fast-food restaurant with my mother. There was a young man begging for money to buy food. I told my mother I was not going to give him money to spend on drugs. She looked at me and said, "The least you can do is buy him a meal. Maybe he's truly hungry. Do you know how many times I was hungry in these streets?" She purchased a meal for the young man and handed it to him with a big smile and said, "I pray you find a way to get out of these streets."

From that day on, I have never denied anyone a meal. Recently, I visited the fish market to buy crabs. This petite woman, who was clearly high as a kite, approached me as I walked inside and asked for a dollar. I told her, "I won't give you a dollar, but I will buy you something to eat." She said, "Anything I want?" I said yes, and she ordered a combo scallop, shrimp, and fish platter with a Coke. When I paid the cashier, the woman approached me and said, "This is the best meal I've had in years. God bless you, sister." I gave her a hug and told her I'd pray for her.

When I got in my car and turned on the radio, I heard the soothing sound of "Reasons" by Earth, Wind & Fire coming from the speakers. Suddenly, I felt a loving presence touch my spirit. In that moment, I knew that my mother was with me, letting me know that she was proud. My mother taught me that small acts of kindness can go a long way to bring happiness to others. I've dedicated my career to giving back. I am now on a journey of sharing my story to inspire others who may be struggling and feeling defeated by the obstacles life has thrown their way. Since I've decided to share my story, I've been overwhelmed with blessings. It's a sign from God that this work matters. Remember, God blesses us so we can bless others. I'm a walking testament to this fact.

## LESSON SEVEN

Always put your faith ahead of your fear! Be unapologetic in embracing your faith and accepting that a higher power is walking with you and has your back. Fear is truly nothing but False Evidence Appearing Real.

My mother was too afraid to deal with a diagnosis of HIV or AIDS, so she turned to crack instead of a doctor to get tested. She had no faith that God would spare her from the diagnosis. She lacked the courage to face her fear head-on.

I have never liked the feeling of fear—that tingling in the pit of my stomach, the increased heart rate, and the feeling of panic upon me. Whenever I get that feeling, I end it immediately by facing it head-on. It always ends up that the thing I was fearful of was truly insignificant. This holds true with my experience with James. Once he got rid of my precious dog, Sheba, and kicked me in the stomach, my fear of him was gone. I saw him for the coward he truly was. It took my mother longer, but once she let go of her fear of James, she never looked back.

During the final stretch of my mother's life, we both came to realize that only God can turn a mess into a message, a test into a testimony, a trial into a triumph, and a victim into a victor! If you've taken away anything from my story, I hope it was to enjoy your life's journey and to be grateful for your blessings. ■